MI BARRIO

from SmarterComics™

MI BARRIO

from SmarterComics™

Based on the book *From the Barrio to the Board Room*

ROBERT RENTERIA

As told to Corey Michael Blake

Illustrated by
Shane Clester

Executive Editor
Corey Michael Blake

Creative Director
Nathan Brown

Adapted by
Shane Clester

Summarized by
Katie Gutierrez-Painter

Writers of the Round Table Press

rtc
A Round Table Companies Production
www.roundtablepress.com

FOREWORD

In our ego-centric society, very rarely are people out for an unselfish, pure, and innocent intention of helping other people. After getting to know Robert Renteria, I recognized he wanted to do something for the betterment of our community. He knows the kids, has walked in their footsteps, and he understands the lack of hope in their eyes. Robert knows firsthand that our kids are rubbing elbows with gang bangers every day in school, and that they'd rather get along with those gang bangers than talk to the police or to a teacher who doesn't look like them or know their culture.

Like Robert, I also understand our children. Most of my elected career has revolved around the betterment of our community on behalf of those who will inherit it…our children. I've watched them shift from a time when they could play outside at all hours, to a modern world where they have to be indoors before the sun goes down for fear of a drive by shooting. When I started getting involved, I was a second-generation board member for the YWCA, and the only Hispanic at the table. Now so many of us — politicians, teachers, lawyers and authors like Robert — are getting involved to make a difference.

I've watched Robert leave an everlasting footprint on kids' lives. He's saying, "Hey that was me once, and now I'm chairman of the board of this company" and "I'm an author" and "I've served our country in the Army." And the kids respond by wanting to change their own lives. He's a positive role model who doesn't want anything from them other than to see them succeed in life.

But it isn't just this generation that Robert and his story are impacting in a positive way. It's potentially every generation of kids throughout the United States and around the world. Inevitably, one of those kids will be the next president, CEO, or teacher that looks like the children that he or she works with, represents, or leads.

When I think about how humbled I am that Robert asked me to do the foreword for his comic book, I think back to my own youth and a time when people near to me called me stupid. They didn't understand why I wanted to read books or go to college or become an Officer in the U.S. Army, because they thought I wasn't smart enough, and that my life would consist of remaining barefoot and pregnant. I had two paths to choose from: the one "they" saw for me, and the one I saw for myself. I chose the latter and worked hard to prove them wrong.

Like me, so many of our kids also have that stamp of failure on them. So many of them are fighting their way through poverty, or they are facing abuse or neglect. Today we have an opportunity to stand together and help them change their direction as mine was changed and as Robert's was changed, thanks to mentors who cared.

I am honored to support Robert Renteria...a mentor. I believe that God has us both here for a reason. I work to inspire change through legislation, and Robert is doing it by sharing his personal story in his books. Children who read this book could have their lives changed forever. The book itself… the story Robert has to tell… can build up any young person's self esteem because they can relate to the trials and tribulations Robert endured.

Put this book in their hands, and something magical can happen. You'll watch our youth envision their true potential. Put this book in their hands, and you'll watch them soar.

Hon. Linda Chapa LaVia
Illinois House of Representatives, 83rd District
Chairperson, Appropriations Committee-Elementary & Secondary Education

Introduction

I am dedicating this comic book to all the children around the world who face any kind of adversity. Regardless of where you come from, the secrets to success are hard work, determination and education. My hope is that *Mi Barrio* will be used as a road map to help inspire and motivate others to avoid the detours that I took in my life. My hope is that *Mi Barrio* will help our youth to find their identity, establish core values, set goals for themselves, prioritize education, and strive to reach their full potential. We cannot allow them to be stripped of their future -- we have the obligation to encourage them to dream big, really big, and then help them pursue those dreams. I believe this book will help to change the landscape for our youth across America by replacing the violence, delinquency, gangs and drugs with education, pride, accomplishment and self esteem.

 I want to give thanks to God for teaching me that wonders never cease -- that a poor little boy coming from the Barrio of East L.A. could one day be a published author. Dreams do come true.

Many thanks to Franco Arda of SmarterComics for sharing my vision, to my publisher Corey Michael Blake for understanding that *From the Barrio to the Board Room* and *Mi Barrio* are not just books and words, but a burning message of hope and dreams. Thank you to my dear friend and fellow board member Cheryl Maraffio for standing with me and believing that together we can make a difference.

A special thank you to Nathan Brown for his creative guidance and to Shane Clester for the fantastic artwork. You've all helped to bring *Barrio* to life so that more children and adults will now see that anything is possible if you believe.

Robert Renteria

"Don't let where you came from dictate who you are,
but let it be part of who you become."

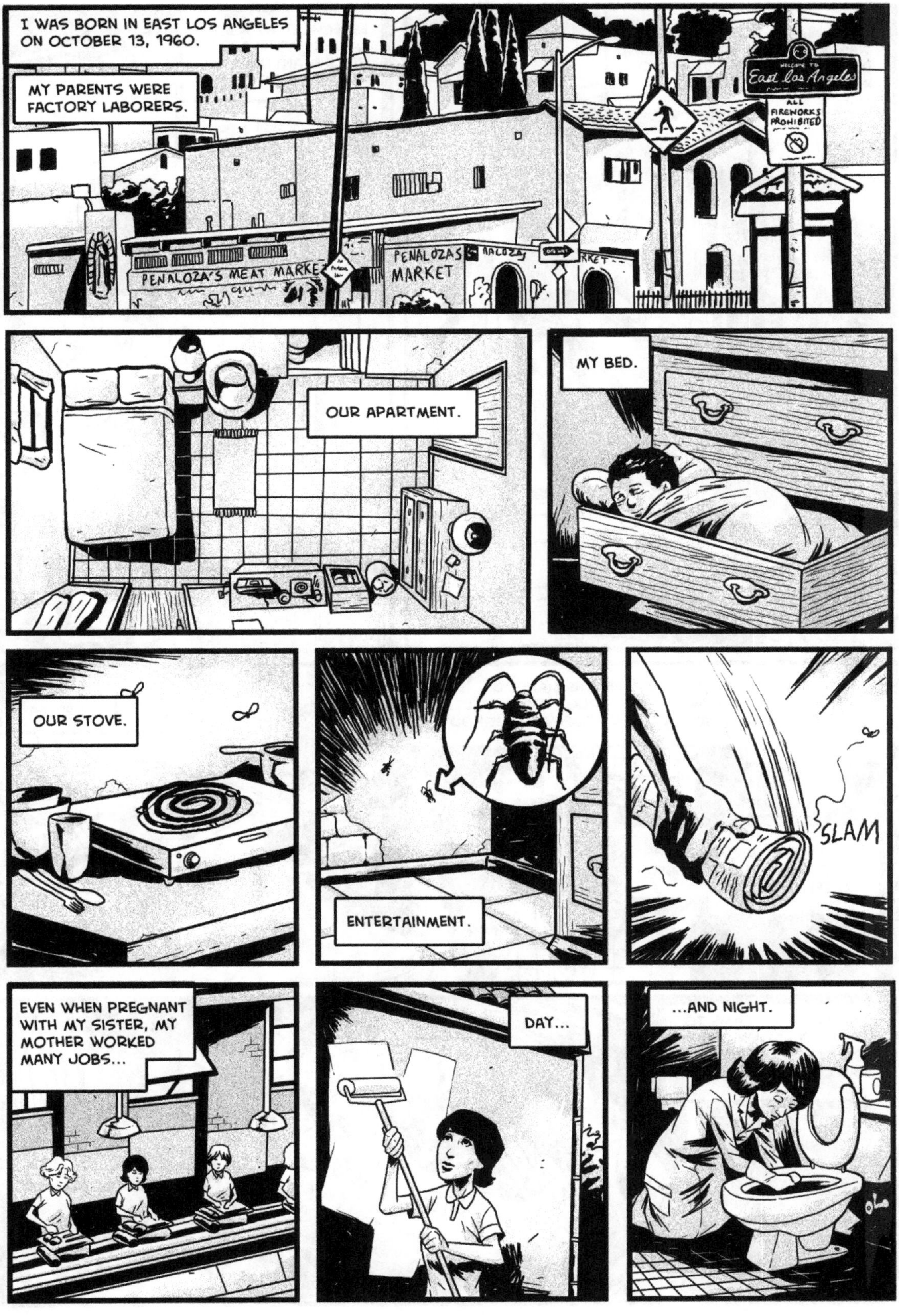
I WAS BORN IN EAST LOS ANGELES ON OCTOBER 13, 1960.
MY PARENTS WERE FACTORY LABORERS.
East Los Angeles
ALL FIREWORKS PROHIBITED
PENALOZA'S MEAT MARKE
PENALOZAS MARKET
OUR APARTMENT.
MY BED.
OUR STOVE.
ENTERTAINMENT.
SLAM
EVEN WHEN PREGNANT WITH MY SISTER, MY MOTHER WORKED MANY JOBS...
DAY...
...AND NIGHT.

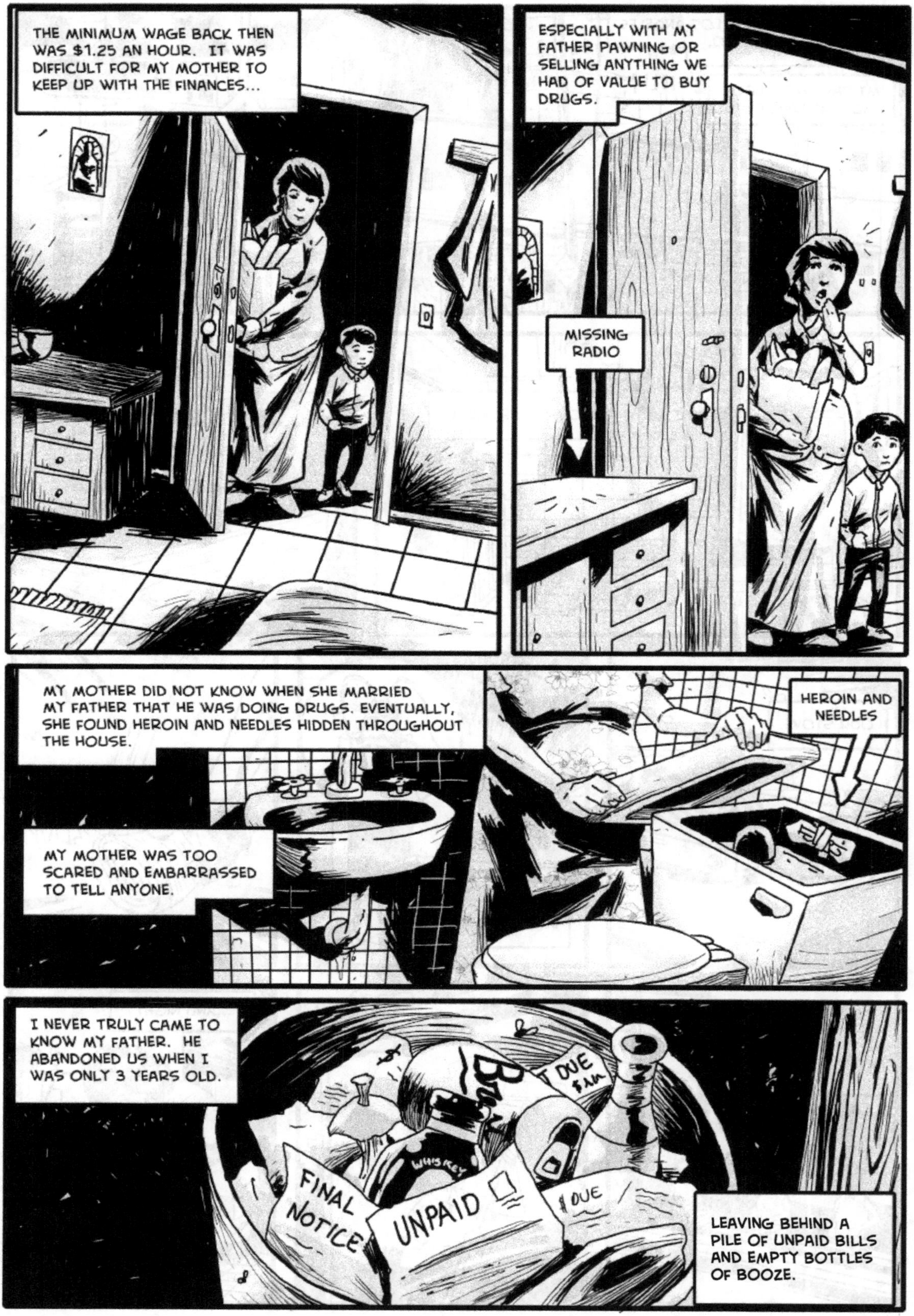
THE MINIMUM WAGE BACK THEN WAS $1.25 AN HOUR. IT WAS DIFFICULT FOR MY MOTHER TO KEEP UP WITH THE FINANCES...
ESPECIALLY WITH MY FATHER PAWNING OR SELLING ANYTHING WE HAD OF VALUE TO BUY DRUGS.
MISSING RADIO
MY MOTHER DID NOT KNOW WHEN SHE MARRIED MY FATHER THAT HE WAS DOING DRUGS. EVENTUALLY, SHE FOUND HEROIN AND NEEDLES HIDDEN THROUGHOUT THE HOUSE.
HEROIN AND NEEDLES
MY MOTHER WAS TOO SCARED AND EMBARRASSED TO TELL ANYONE.
I NEVER TRULY CAME TO KNOW MY FATHER. HE ABANDONED US WHEN I WAS ONLY 3 YEARS OLD.
DUE
WHISKEY
FINAL NOTICE
UNPAID
$ DUE
LEAVING BEHIND A PILE OF UNPAID BILLS AND EMPTY BOTTLES OF BOOZE.

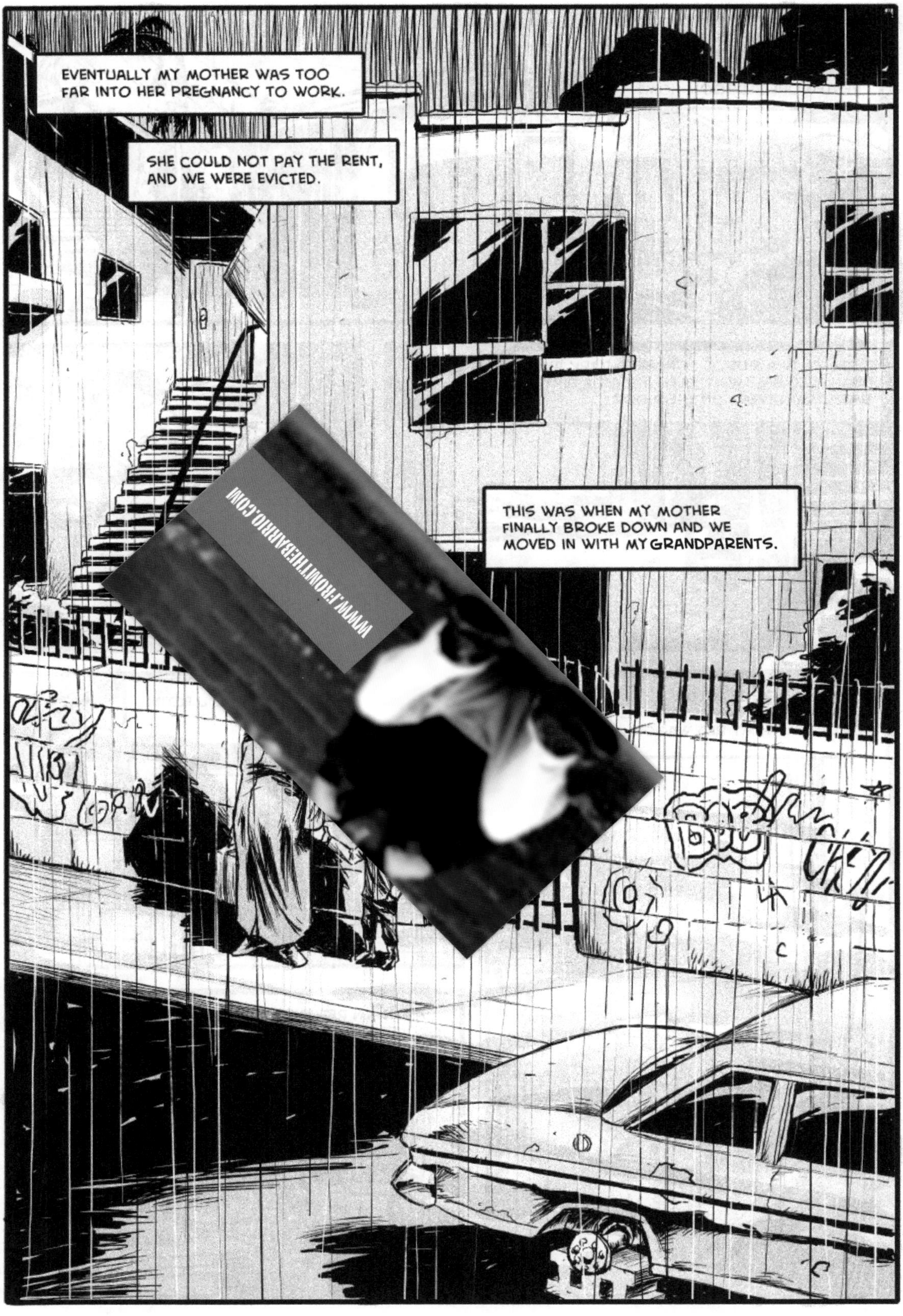
EVENTUALLY MY MOTHER WAS TOO FAR INTO HER PREGNANCY TO WORK.
SHE COULD NOT PAY THE RENT, AND WE WERE EVICTED.
THIS WAS WHEN MY MOTHER FINALLY BROKE DOWN AND WE MOVED IN WITH MY GRANDPARENTS.
WWW.FROMTHEBARRIO.COM

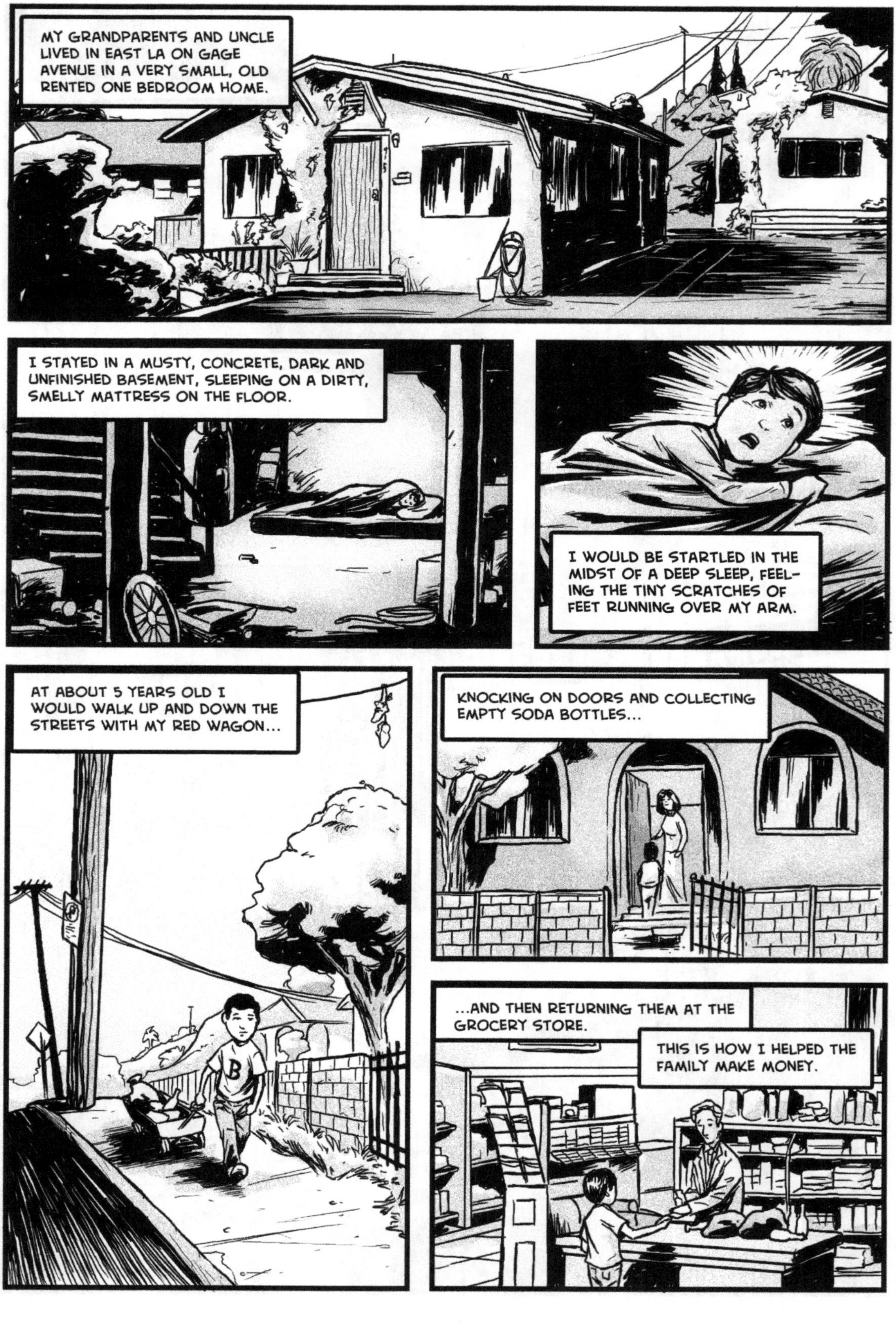
MY GRANDPARENTS AND UNCLE LIVED IN EAST LA ON GAGE AVENUE IN A VERY SMALL, OLD RENTED ONE BEDROOM HOME.
I STAYED IN A MUSTY, CONCRETE, DARK AND UNFINISHED BASEMENT, SLEEPING ON A DIRTY, SMELLY MATTRESS ON THE FLOOR.
I WOULD BE STARTLED IN THE MIDST OF A DEEP SLEEP, FEEL-ING THE TINY SCRATCHES OF FEET RUNNING OVER MY ARM.
AT ABOUT 5 YEARS OLD I WOULD WALK UP AND DOWN THE STREETS WITH MY RED WAGON...
KNOCKING ON DOORS AND COLLECTING EMPTY SODA BOTTLES...
...AND THEN RETURNING THEM AT THE GROCERY STORE.
THIS IS HOW I HELPED THE FAMILY MAKE MONEY.

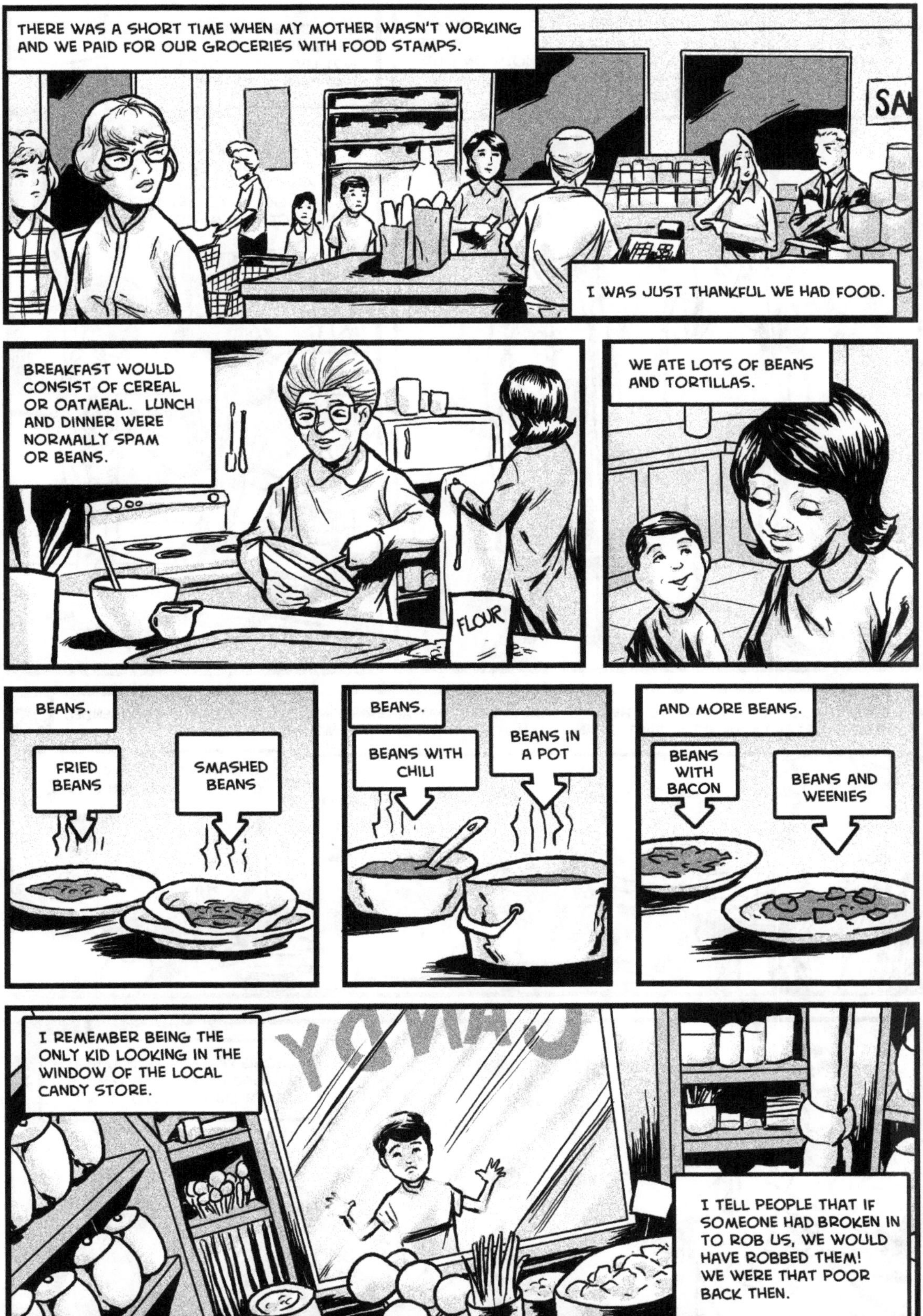
THERE WAS A SHORT TIME WHEN MY MOTHER WASN'T WORKING AND WE PAID FOR OUR GROCERIES WITH FOOD STAMPS.
SA
I WAS JUST THANKFUL WE HAD FOOD.
BREAKFAST WOULD CONSIST OF CEREAL OR OATMEAL. LUNCH AND DINNER WERE NORMALLY SPAM OR BEANS.
FLOUR
WE ATE LOTS OF BEANS AND TORTILLAS.
BEANS.
FRIED BEANS
SMASHED BEANS
BEANS.
BEANS WITH CHILI
BEANS IN A POT
AND MORE BEANS.
BEANS WITH BACON
BEANS AND WEENIES
CANDY
I REMEMBER BEING THE ONLY KID LOOKING IN THE WINDOW OF THE LOCAL CANDY STORE.
I TELL PEOPLE THAT IF SOMEONE HAD BROKEN IN TO ROB US, WE WOULD HAVE ROBBED THEM! WE WERE THAT POOR BACK THEN.

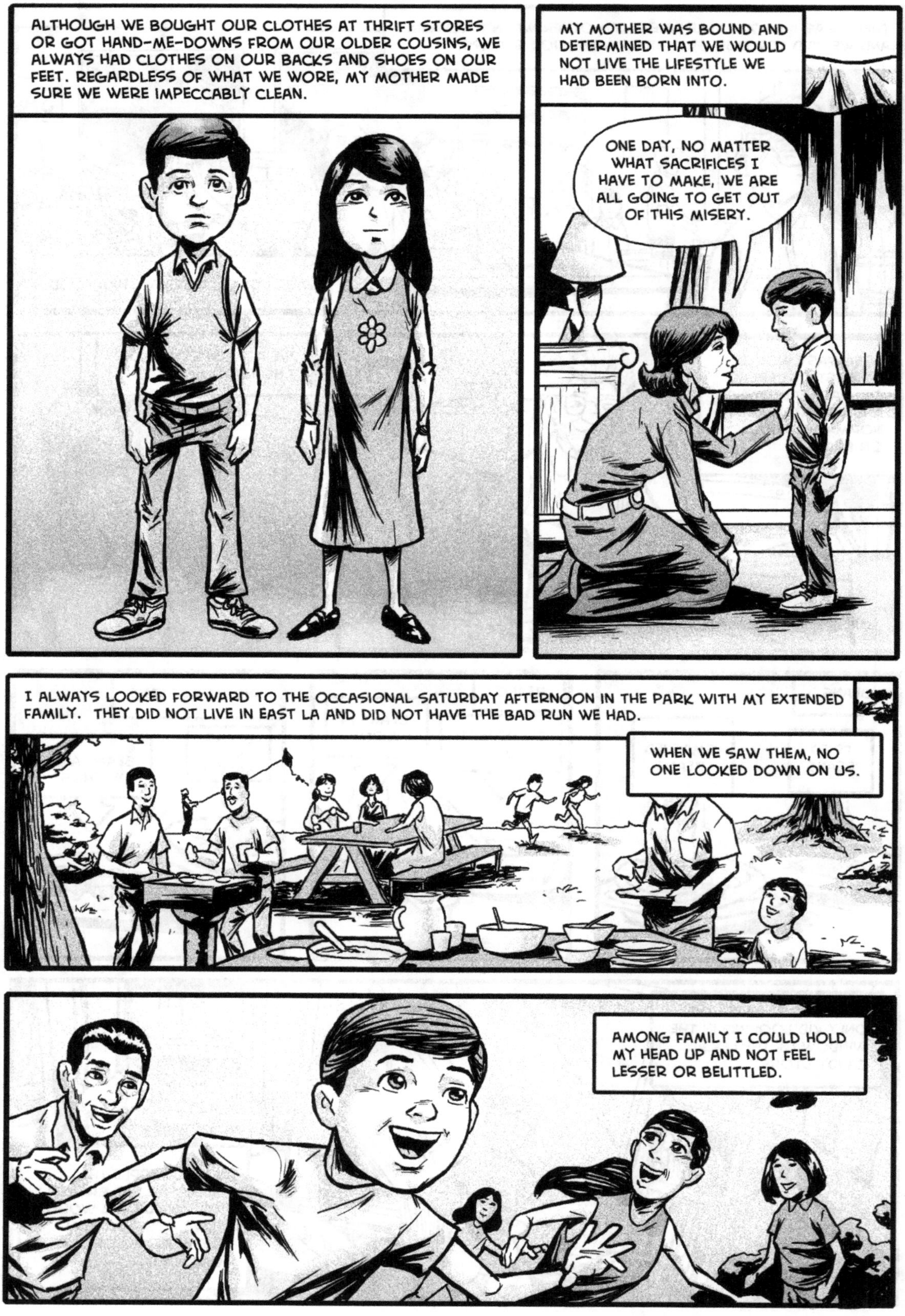
ALTHOUGH WE BOUGHT OUR CLOTHES AT THRIFT STORES OR GOT HAND-ME-DOWNS FROM OUR OLDER COUSINS, WE ALWAYS HAD CLOTHES ON OUR BACKS AND SHOES ON OUR FEET. REGARDLESS OF WHAT WE WORE, MY MOTHER MADE SURE WE WERE IMPECCABLY CLEAN.
MY MOTHER WAS BOUND AND DETERMINED THAT WE WOULD NOT LIVE THE LIFESTYLE WE HAD BEEN BORN INTO.
ONE DAY, NO MATTER WHAT SACRIFICES I HAVE TO MAKE, WE ARE ALL GOING TO GET OUT OF THIS MISERY.
I ALWAYS LOOKED FORWARD TO THE OCCASIONAL SATURDAY AFTERNOON IN THE PARK WITH MY EXTENDED FAMILY. THEY DID NOT LIVE IN EAST LA AND DID NOT HAVE THE BAD RUN WE HAD.
WHEN WE SAW THEM, NO ONE LOOKED DOWN ON US.
AMONG FAMILY I COULD HOLD MY HEAD UP AND NOT FEEL LESSER OR BELITTLED.

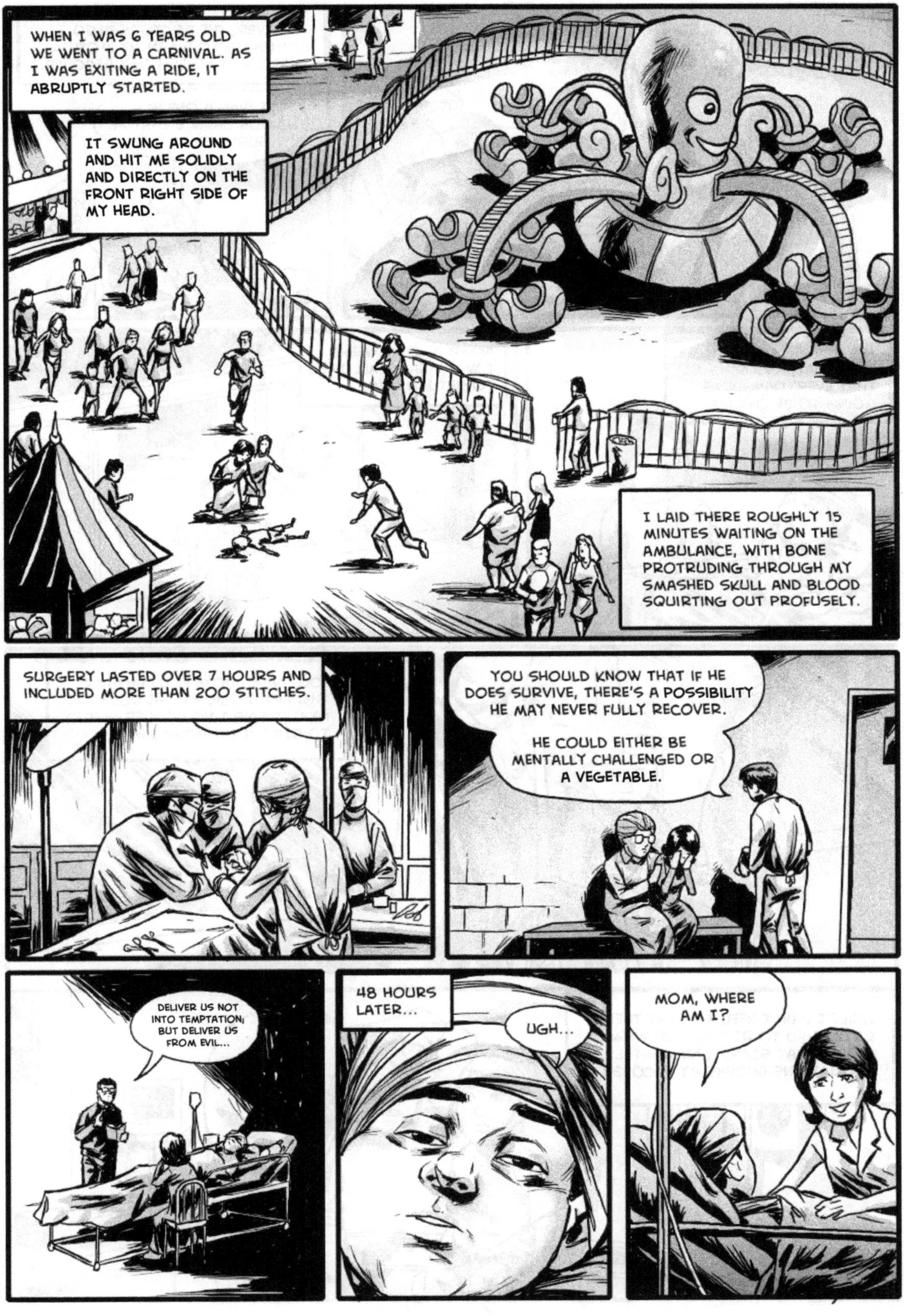

WHEN I WAS 6 YEARS OLD WE WENT TO A CARNIVAL. AS I WAS EXITING A RIDE, IT ABRUPTLY STARTED.
IT SWUNG AROUND AND HIT ME SOLIDLY AND DIRECTLY ON THE FRONT RIGHT SIDE OF MY HEAD.
I LAID THERE ROUGHLY 15 MINUTES WAITING ON THE AMBULANCE, WITH BONE PROTRUDING THROUGH MY SMASHED SKULL AND BLOOD SQUIRTING OUT PROFUSELY.
SURGERY LASTED OVER 7 HOURS AND INCLUDED MORE THAN 200 STITCHES.
YOU SHOULD KNOW THAT IF HE DOES SURVIVE, THERE'S A POSSIBILITY HE MAY NEVER FULLY RECOVER.
HE COULD EITHER BE MENTALLY CHALLENGED OR A VEGETABLE.
DELIVER US NOT INTO TEMPTATION; BUT DELIVER US FROM EVIL...
48 HOURS LATER...
UGH...
MOM, WHERE AM I?

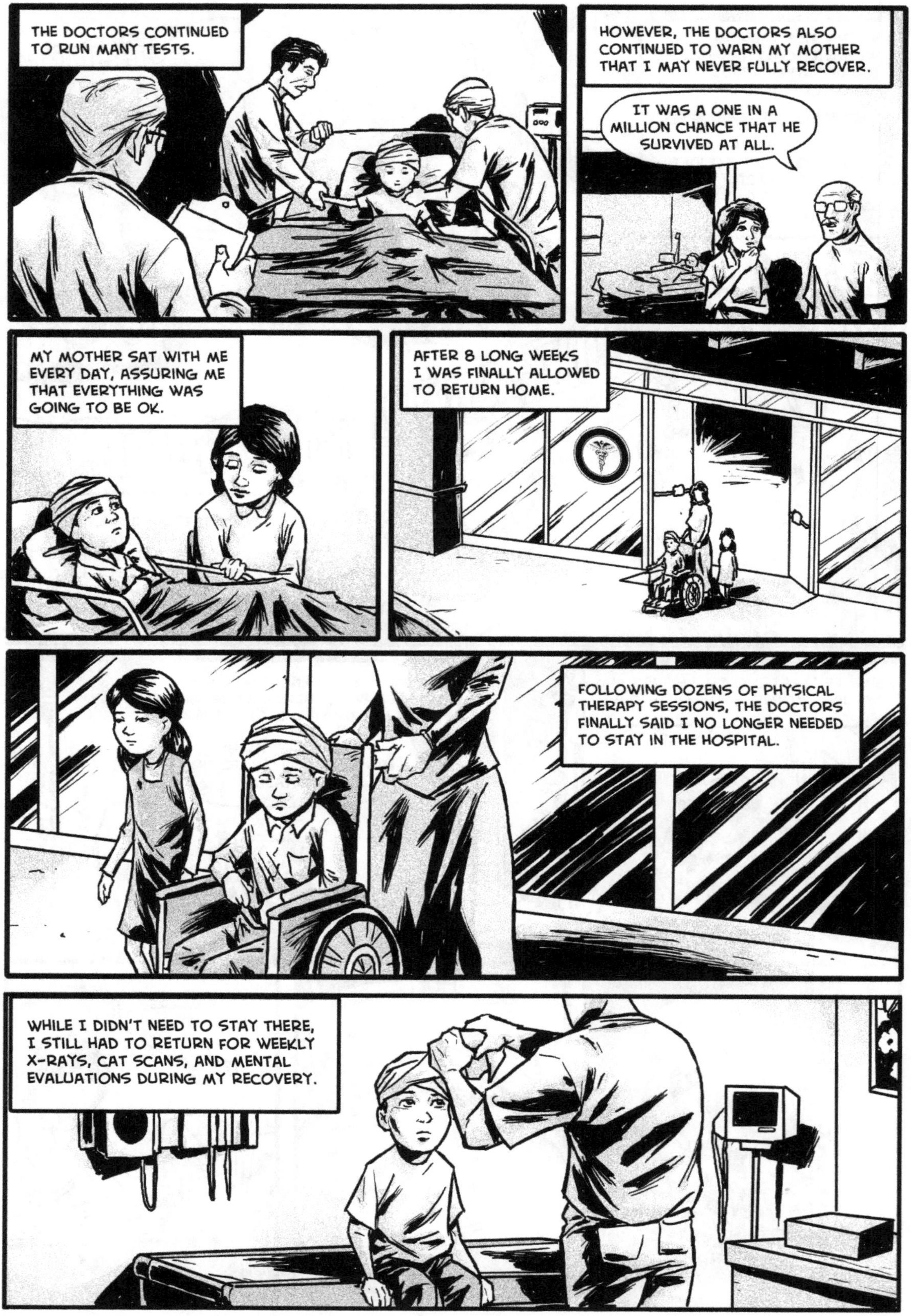
THE DOCTORS CONTINUED TO RUN MANY TESTS.
HOWEVER, THE DOCTORS ALSO CONTINUED TO WARN MY MOTHER THAT I MAY NEVER FULLY RECOVER.
IT WAS A ONE IN A MILLION CHANCE THAT HE SURVIVED AT ALL.
MY MOTHER SAT WITH ME EVERY DAY, ASSURING ME THAT EVERYTHING WAS GOING TO BE OK.
AFTER 8 LONG WEEKS I WAS FINALLY ALLOWED TO RETURN HOME.
FOLLOWING DOZENS OF PHYSICAL THERAPY SESSIONS, THE DOCTORS FINALLY SAID I NO LONGER NEEDED TO STAY IN THE HOSPITAL.
WHILE I DIDN'T NEED TO STAY THERE, I STILL HAD TO RETURN FOR WEEKLY X-RAYS, CAT SCANS, AND MENTAL EVALUATIONS DURING MY RECOVERY.

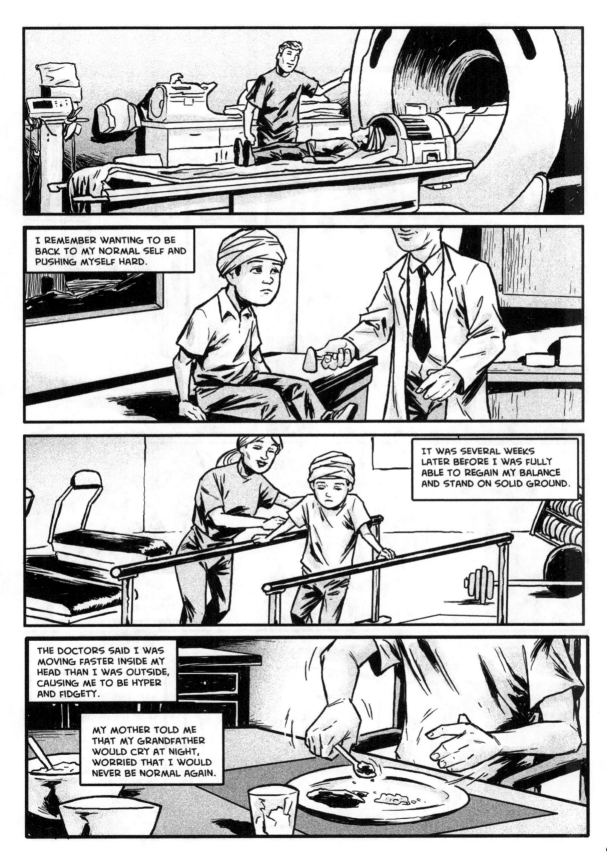

I REMEMBER WANTING TO BE BACK TO MY NORMAL SELF AND PUSHING MYSELF HARD.

IT WAS SEVERAL WEEKS LATER BEFORE I WAS FULLY ABLE TO REGAIN MY BALANCE AND STAND ON SOLID GROUND.

THE DOCTORS SAID I WAS MOVING FASTER INSIDE MY HEAD THAN I WAS OUTSIDE, CAUSING ME TO BE HYPER AND FIDGETY.

MY MOTHER TOLD ME THAT MY GRANDFATHER WOULD CRY AT NIGHT, WORRIED THAT I WOULD NEVER BE NORMAL AGAIN.

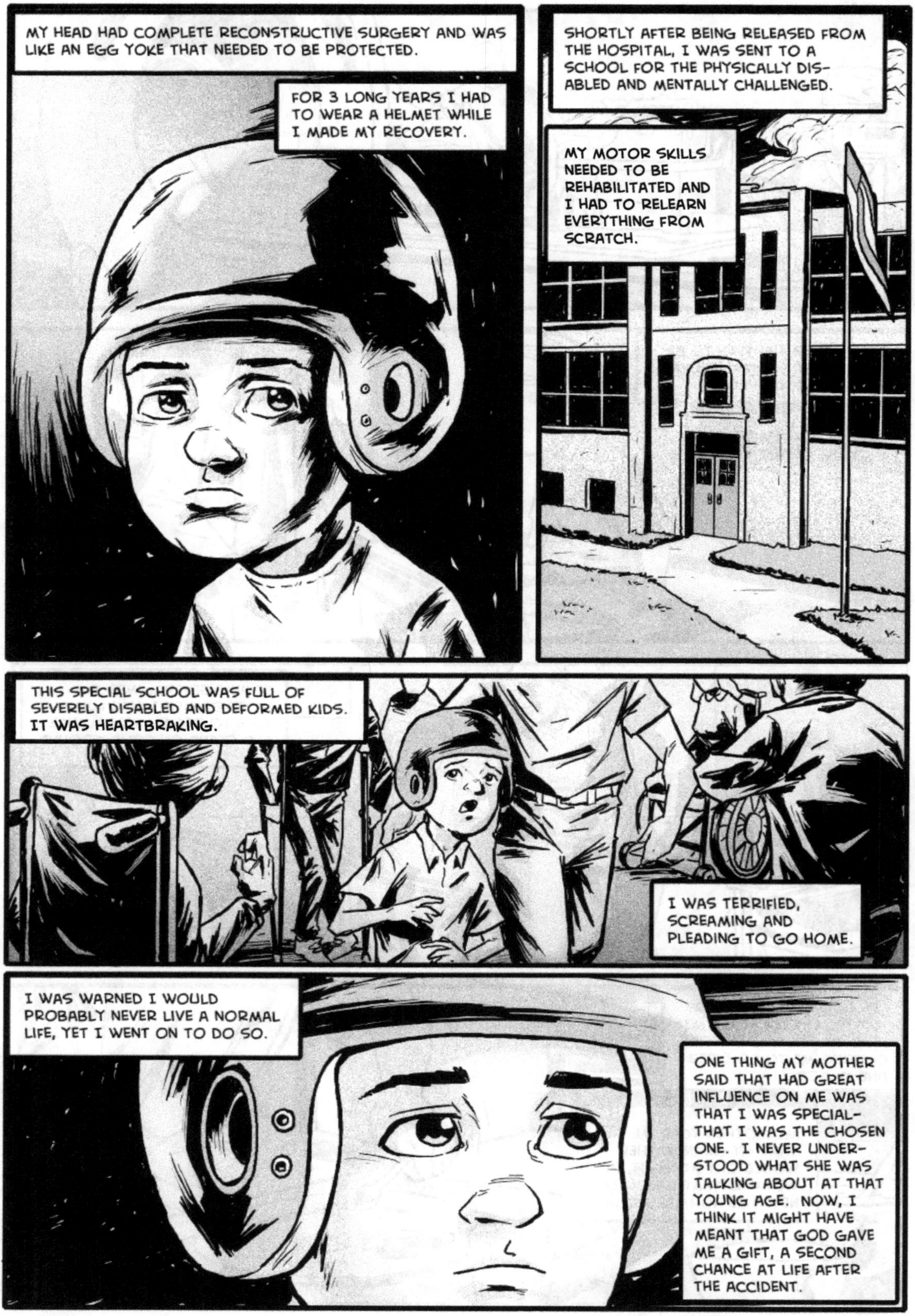
MY HEAD HAD COMPLETE RECONSTRUCTIVE SURGERY AND WAS LIKE AN EGG YOKE THAT NEEDED TO BE PROTECTED.
FOR 3 LONG YEARS I HAD TO WEAR A HELMET WHILE I MADE MY RECOVERY.
SHORTLY AFTER BEING RELEASED FROM THE HOSPITAL, I WAS SENT TO A SCHOOL FOR THE PHYSICALLY DIS-ABLED AND MENTALLY CHALLENGED.
MY MOTOR SKILLS NEEDED TO BE REHABILITATED AND I HAD TO RELEARN EVERYTHING FROM SCRATCH.
THIS SPECIAL SCHOOL WAS FULL OF SEVERELY DISABLED AND DEFORMED KIDS. IT WAS HEARTBRAKING.
I WAS TERRIFIED, SCREAMING AND PLEADING TO GO HOME.
I WAS WARNED I WOULD PROBABLY NEVER LIVE A NORMAL LIFE, YET I WENT ON TO DO SO.
ONE THING MY MOTHER SAID THAT HAD GREAT INFLUENCE ON ME WAS THAT I WAS SPECIAL- THAT I WAS THE CHOSEN ONE. I NEVER UNDER-STOOD WHAT SHE WAS TALKING ABOUT AT THAT YOUNG AGE. NOW, I THINK IT MIGHT HAVE MEANT THAT GOD GAVE ME A GIFT, A SECOND CHANCE AT LIFE AFTER THE ACCIDENT.

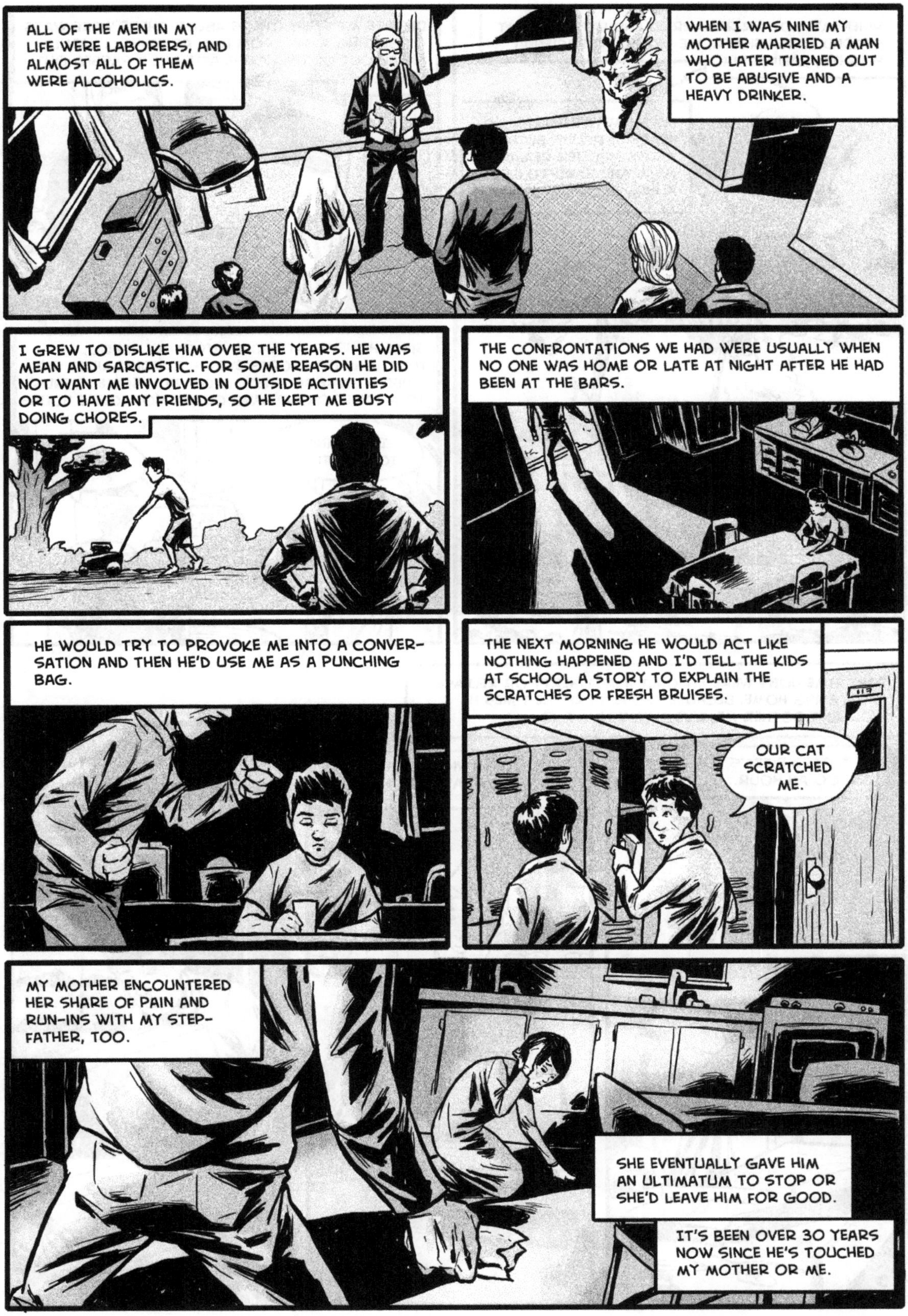
ALL OF THE MEN IN MY LIFE WERE LABORERS, AND ALMOST ALL OF THEM WERE ALCOHOLICS.
WHEN I WAS NINE MY MOTHER MARRIED A MAN WHO LATER TURNED OUT TO BE ABUSIVE AND A HEAVY DRINKER.
I GREW TO DISLIKE HIM OVER THE YEARS. HE WAS MEAN AND SARCASTIC. FOR SOME REASON HE DID NOT WANT ME INVOLVED IN OUTSIDE ACTIVITIES OR TO HAVE ANY FRIENDS, SO HE KEPT ME BUSY DOING CHORES.
THE CONFRONTATIONS WE HAD WERE USUALLY WHEN NO ONE WAS HOME OR LATE AT NIGHT AFTER HE HAD BEEN AT THE BARS.
HE WOULD TRY TO PROVOKE ME INTO A CONVERSATION AND THEN HE'D USE ME AS A PUNCHING BAG.
THE NEXT MORNING HE WOULD ACT LIKE NOTHING HAPPENED AND I'D TELL THE KIDS AT SCHOOL A STORY TO EXPLAIN THE SCRATCHES OR FRESH BRUISES.
OUR CAT SCRATCHED ME.
MY MOTHER ENCOUNTERED HER SHARE OF PAIN AND RUN-INS WITH MY STEP-FATHER, TOO.
SHE EVENTUALLY GAVE HIM AN ULTIMATUM TO STOP OR SHE'D LEAVE HIM FOR GOOD.
IT'S BEEN OVER 30 YEARS NOW SINCE HE'S TOUCHED MY MOTHER OR ME.

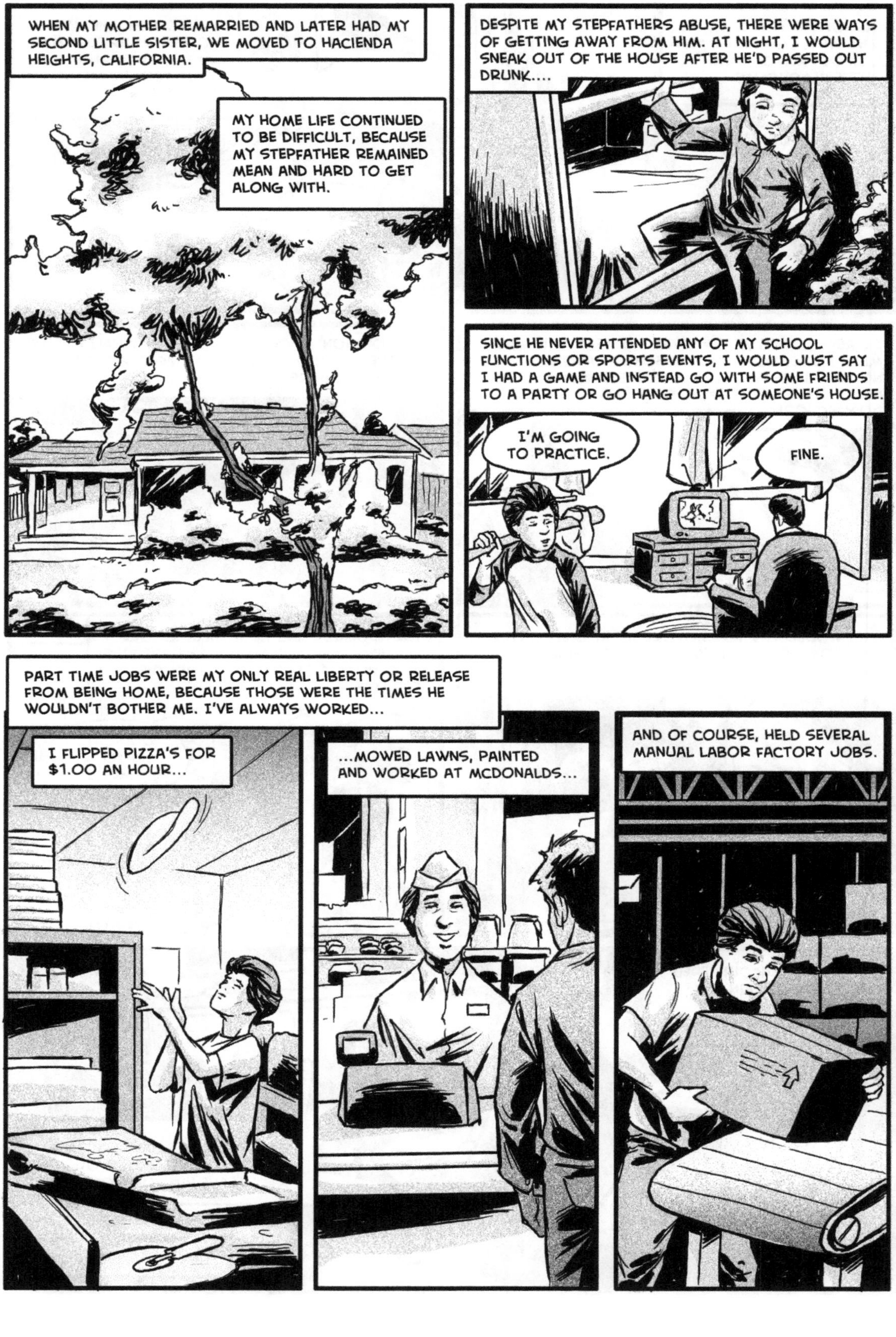
WHEN MY MOTHER REMARRIED AND LATER HAD MY SECOND LITTLE SISTER, WE MOVED TO HACIENDA HEIGHTS, CALIFORNIA.
MY HOME LIFE CONTINUED TO BE DIFFICULT, BECAUSE MY STEPFATHER REMAINED MEAN AND HARD TO GET ALONG WITH.
DESPITE MY STEPFATHERS ABUSE, THERE WERE WAYS OF GETTING AWAY FROM HIM. AT NIGHT, I WOULD SNEAK OUT OF THE HOUSE AFTER HE'D PASSED OUT DRUNK....
SINCE HE NEVER ATTENDED ANY OF MY SCHOOL FUNCTIONS OR SPORTS EVENTS, I WOULD JUST SAY I HAD A GAME AND INSTEAD GO WITH SOME FRIENDS TO A PARTY OR GO HANG OUT AT SOMEONE'S HOUSE.
I'M GOING TO PRACTICE.
FINE.
PART TIME JOBS WERE MY ONLY REAL LIBERTY OR RELEASE FROM BEING HOME, BECAUSE THOSE WERE THE TIMES HE WOULDN'T BOTHER ME. I'VE ALWAYS WORKED...
I FLIPPED PIZZA'S FOR $1.00 AN HOUR...
...MOWED LAWNS, PAINTED AND WORKED AT MCDONALDS...
AND OF COURSE, HELD SEVERAL MANUAL LABOR FACTORY JOBS.

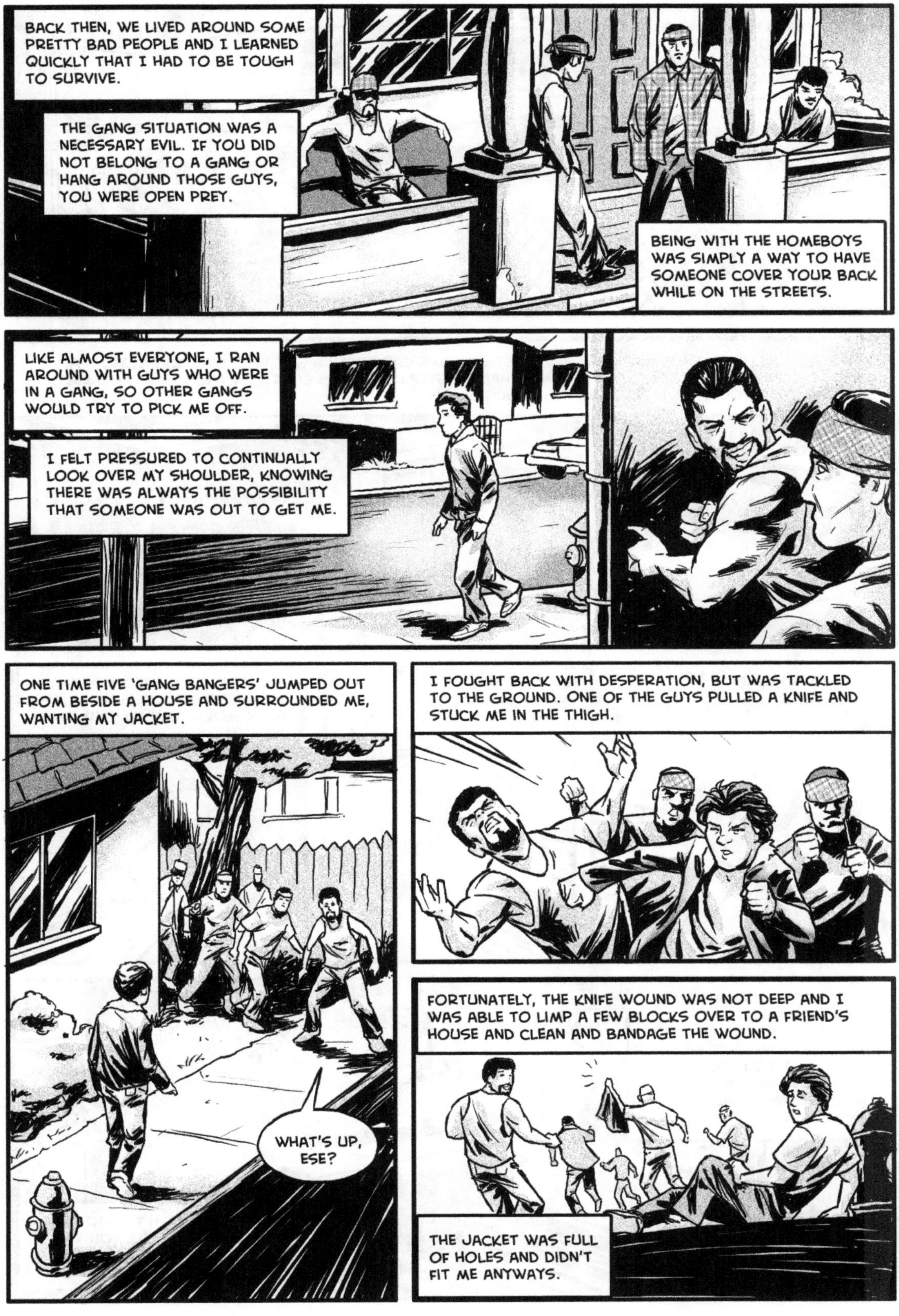

BACK THEN, WE LIVED AROUND SOME PRETTY BAD PEOPLE AND I LEARNED QUICKLY THAT I HAD TO BE TOUGH TO SURVIVE.
THE GANG SITUATION WAS A NECESSARY EVIL. IF YOU DID NOT BELONG TO A GANG OR HANG AROUND THOSE GUYS, YOU WERE OPEN PREY.
BEING WITH THE HOMEBOYS WAS SIMPLY A WAY TO HAVE SOMEONE COVER YOUR BACK WHILE ON THE STREETS.
LIKE ALMOST EVERYONE, I RAN AROUND WITH GUYS WHO WERE IN A GANG, SO OTHER GANGS WOULD TRY TO PICK ME OFF.
I FELT PRESSURED TO CONTINUALLY LOOK OVER MY SHOULDER, KNOWING THERE WAS ALWAYS THE POSSIBILITY THAT SOMEONE WAS OUT TO GET ME.
ONE TIME FIVE 'GANG BANGERS' JUMPED OUT FROM BESIDE A HOUSE AND SURROUNDED ME, WANTING MY JACKET.
WHAT'S UP, ESE?
I FOUGHT BACK WITH DESPERATION, BUT WAS TACKLED TO THE GROUND. ONE OF THE GUYS PULLED A KNIFE AND STUCK ME IN THE THIGH.
FORTUNATELY, THE KNIFE WOUND WAS NOT DEEP AND I WAS ABLE TO LIMP A FEW BLOCKS OVER TO A FRIEND'S HOUSE AND CLEAN AND BANDAGE THE WOUND.
THE JACKET WAS FULL OF HOLES AND DIDN'T FIT ME ANYWAYS.

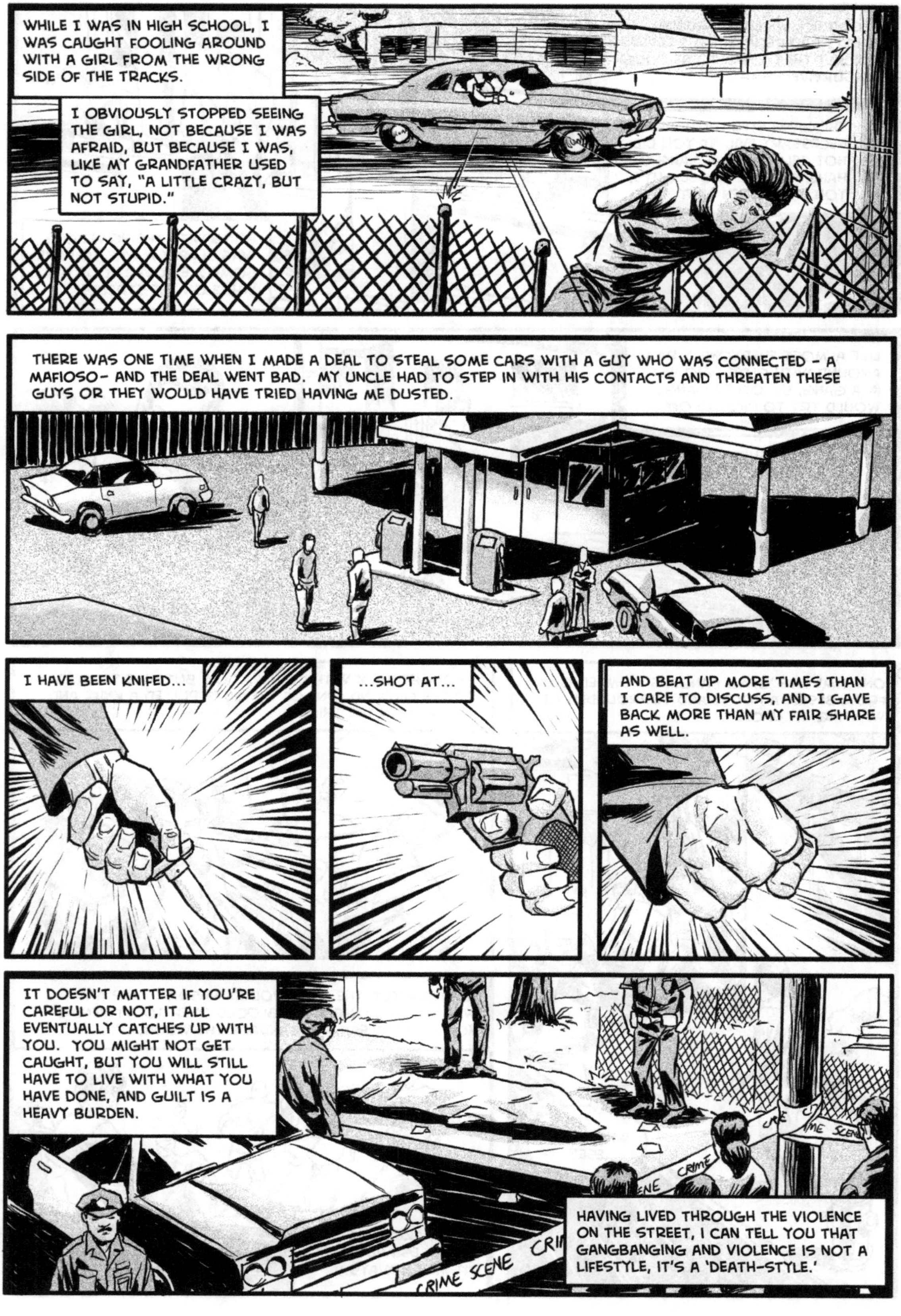
WHILE I WAS IN HIGH SCHOOL, I WAS CAUGHT FOOLING AROUND WITH A GIRL FROM THE WRONG SIDE OF THE TRACKS.
I OBVIOUSLY STOPPED SEEING THE GIRL, NOT BECAUSE I WAS AFRAID, BUT BECAUSE I WAS, LIKE MY GRANDFATHER USED TO SAY, "A LITTLE CRAZY, BUT NOT STUPID."
THERE WAS ONE TIME WHEN I MADE A DEAL TO STEAL SOME CARS WITH A GUY WHO WAS CONNECTED - A MAFIOSO- AND THE DEAL WENT BAD. MY UNCLE HAD TO STEP IN WITH HIS CONTACTS AND THREATEN THESE GUYS OR THEY WOULD HAVE TRIED HAVING ME DUSTED.
I HAVE BEEN KNIFED...
...SHOT AT...
AND BEAT UP MORE TIMES THAN I CARE TO DISCUSS, AND I GAVE BACK MORE THAN MY FAIR SHARE AS WELL.
IT DOESN'T MATTER IF YOU'RE CAREFUL OR NOT, IT ALL EVENTUALLY CATCHES UP WITH YOU. YOU MIGHT NOT GET CAUGHT, BUT YOU WILL STILL HAVE TO LIVE WITH WHAT YOU HAVE DONE, AND GUILT IS A HEAVY BURDEN.
CRIME SCENE
HAVING LIVED THROUGH THE VIOLENCE ON THE STREET, I CAN TELL YOU THAT GANGBANGING AND VIOLENCE IS NOT A LIFESTYLE, IT'S A 'DEATH-STYLE.'

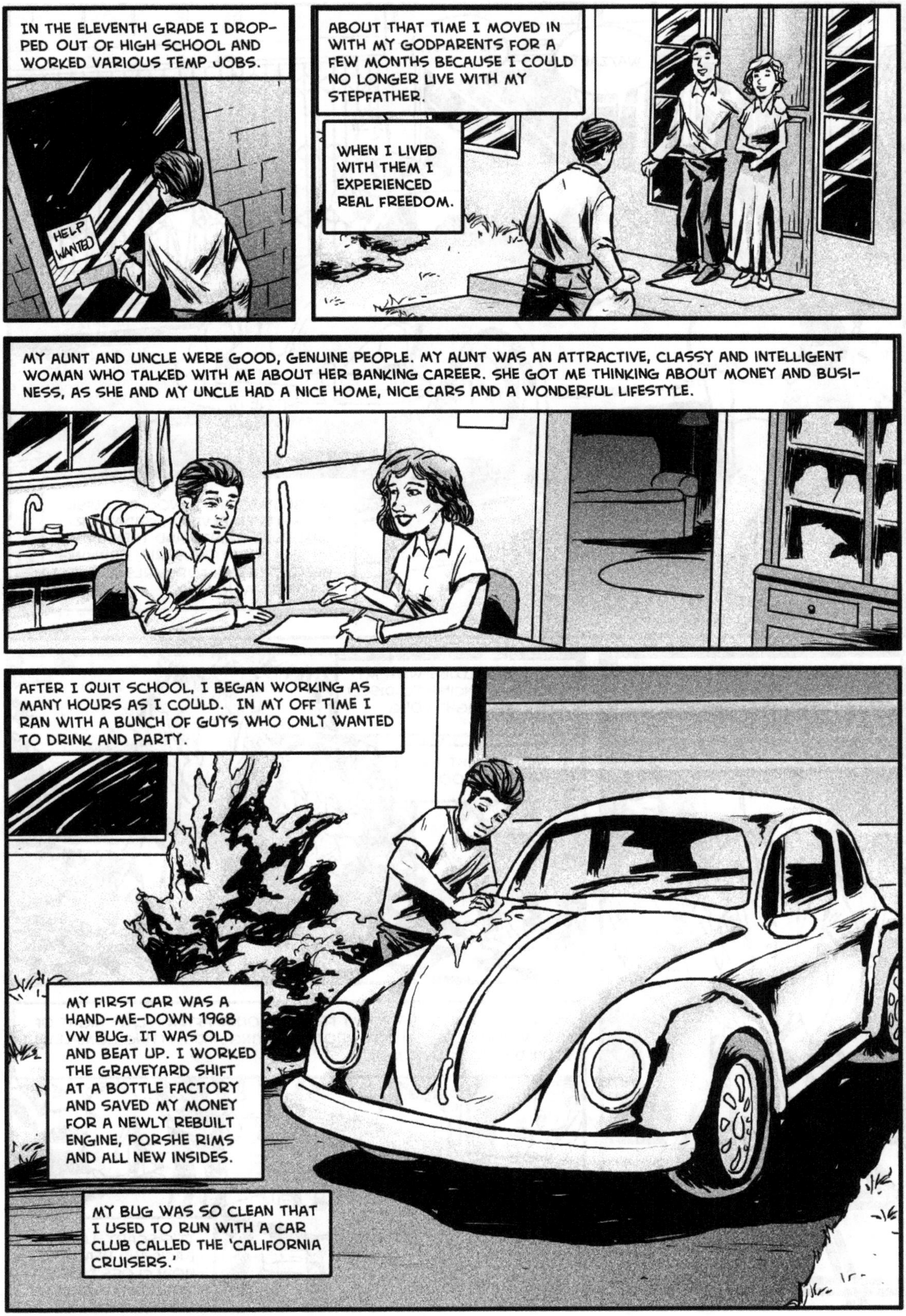
IN THE ELEVENTH GRADE I DROPPED OUT OF HIGH SCHOOL AND WORKED VARIOUS TEMP JOBS.
HELP WANTED
ABOUT THAT TIME I MOVED IN WITH MY GODPARENTS FOR A FEW MONTHS BECAUSE I COULD NO LONGER LIVE WITH MY STEPFATHER.
WHEN I LIVED WITH THEM I EXPERIENCED REAL FREEDOM.
MY AUNT AND UNCLE WERE GOOD, GENUINE PEOPLE. MY AUNT WAS AN ATTRACTIVE, CLASSY AND INTELLIGENT WOMAN WHO TALKED WITH ME ABOUT HER BANKING CAREER. SHE GOT ME THINKING ABOUT MONEY AND BUSINESS, AS SHE AND MY UNCLE HAD A NICE HOME, NICE CARS AND A WONDERFUL LIFESTYLE.
AFTER I QUIT SCHOOL, I BEGAN WORKING AS MANY HOURS AS I COULD. IN MY OFF TIME I RAN WITH A BUNCH OF GUYS WHO ONLY WANTED TO DRINK AND PARTY.
MY FIRST CAR WAS A HAND-ME-DOWN 1968 VW BUG. IT WAS OLD AND BEAT UP. I WORKED THE GRAVEYARD SHIFT AT A BOTTLE FACTORY AND SAVED MY MONEY FOR A NEWLY REBUILT ENGINE, PORSHE RIMS AND ALL NEW INSIDES.
MY BUG WAS SO CLEAN THAT I USED TO RUN WITH A CAR CLUB CALLED THE 'CALIFORNIA CRUISERS.'

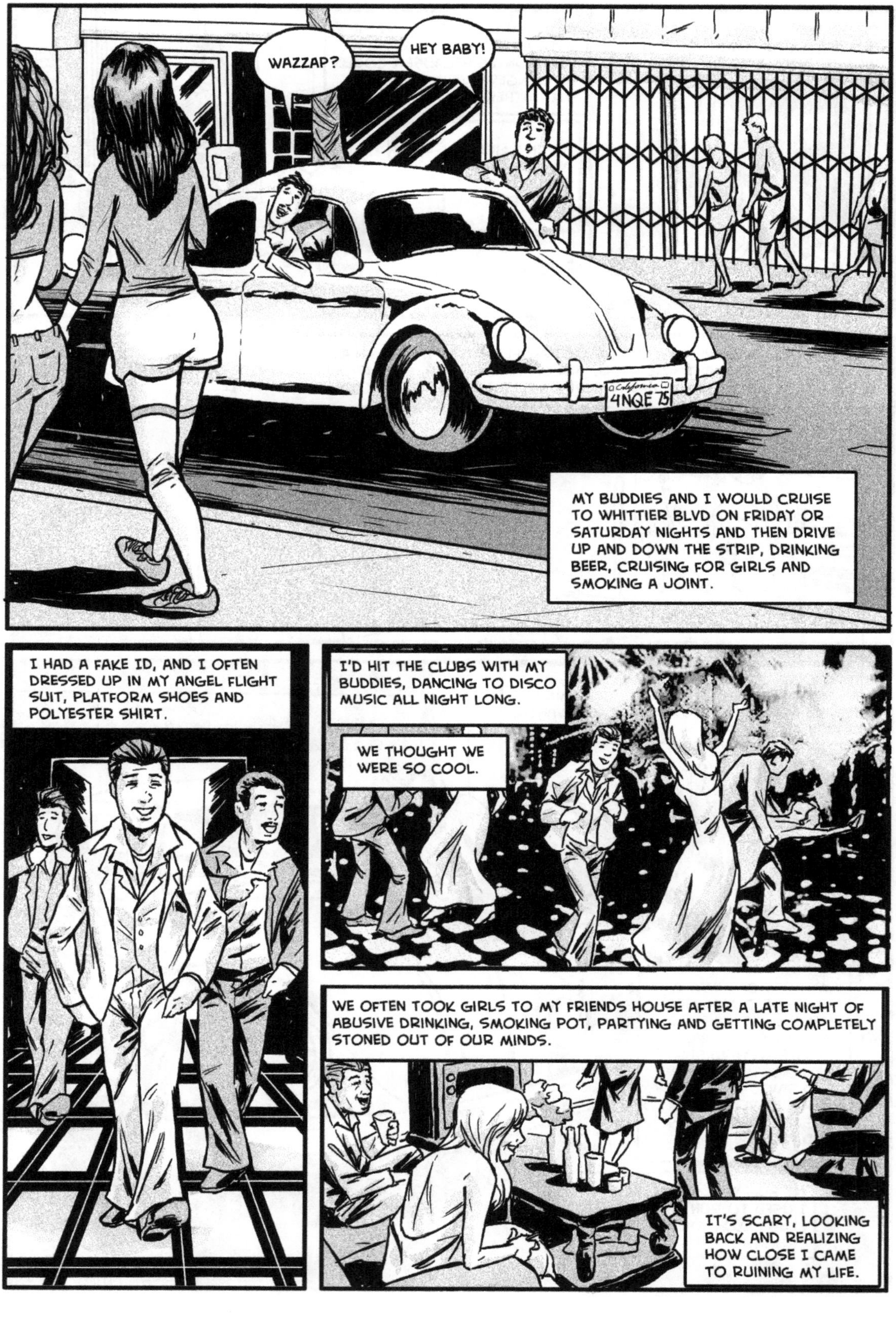

WAZZAP?
HEY BABY!
4NQE 75
MY BUDDIES AND I WOULD CRUISE TO WHITTIER BLVD ON FRIDAY OR SATURDAY NIGHTS AND THEN DRIVE UP AND DOWN THE STRIP, DRINKING BEER, CRUISING FOR GIRLS AND SMOKING A JOINT.
I HAD A FAKE ID, AND I OFTEN DRESSED UP IN MY ANGEL FLIGHT SUIT, PLATFORM SHOES AND POLYESTER SHIRT.
I'D HIT THE CLUBS WITH MY BUDDIES, DANCING TO DISCO MUSIC ALL NIGHT LONG.
WE THOUGHT WE WERE SO COOL.
WE OFTEN TOOK GIRLS TO MY FRIENDS HOUSE AFTER A LATE NIGHT OF ABUSIVE DRINKING, SMOKING POT, PARTYING AND GETTING COMPLETELY STONED OUT OF OUR MINDS.
IT'S SCARY, LOOKING BACK AND REALIZING HOW CLOSE I CAME TO RUINING MY LIFE.

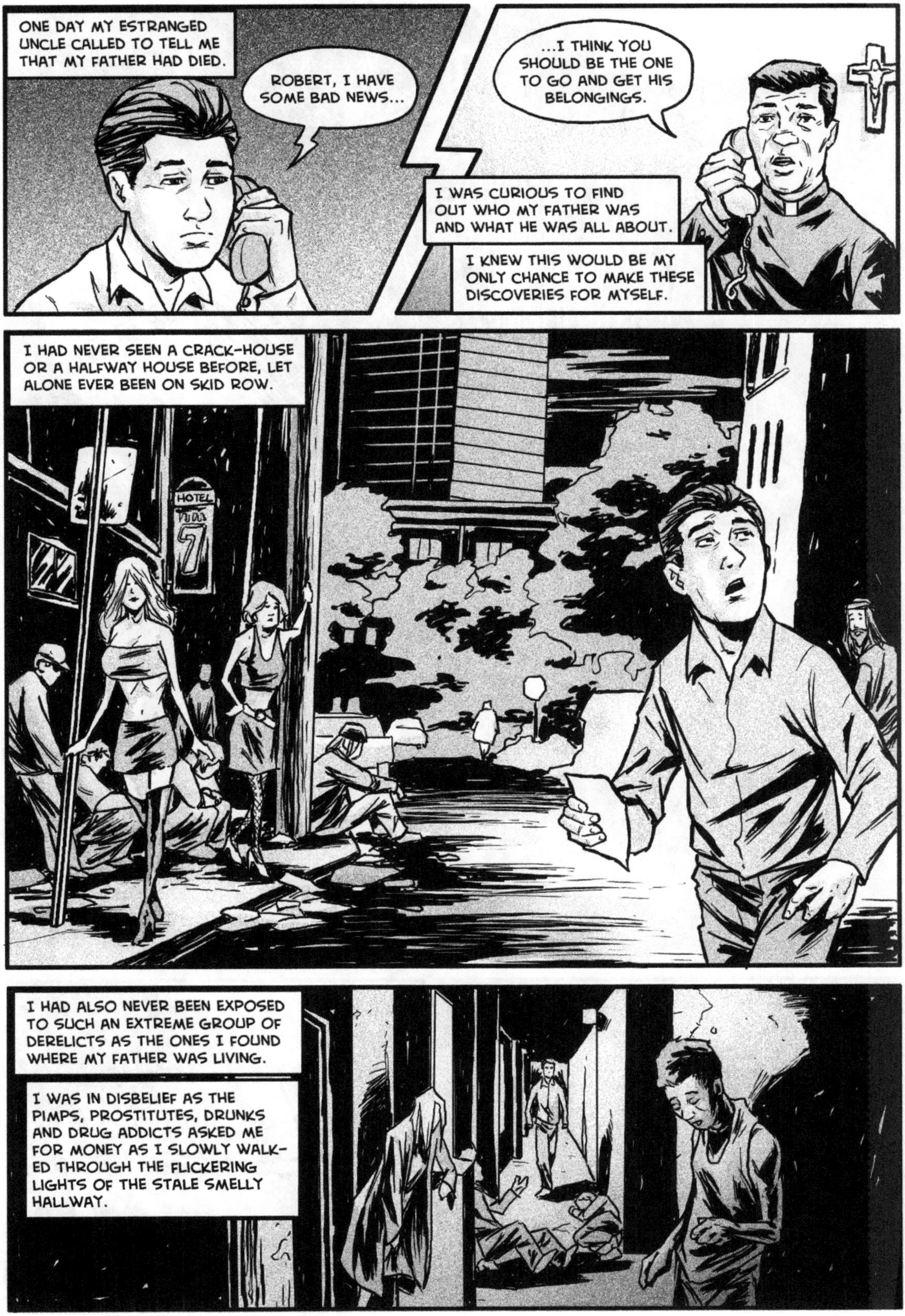

ONE DAY MY ESTRANGED UNCLE CALLED TO TELL ME THAT MY FATHER HAD DIED.
ROBERT, I HAVE SOME BAD NEWS...
...I THINK YOU SHOULD BE THE ONE TO GO AND GET HIS BELONGINGS.
I WAS CURIOUS TO FIND OUT WHO MY FATHER WAS AND WHAT HE WAS ALL ABOUT.
I KNEW THIS WOULD BE MY ONLY CHANCE TO MAKE THESE DISCOVERIES FOR MYSELF.
I HAD NEVER SEEN A CRACK-HOUSE OR A HALFWAY HOUSE BEFORE, LET ALONE EVER BEEN ON SKID ROW.
HOTEL
7
I HAD ALSO NEVER BEEN EXPOSED TO SUCH AN EXTREME GROUP OF DERELICTS AS THE ONES I FOUND WHERE MY FATHER WAS LIVING.
I WAS IN DISBELIEF AS THE PIMPS, PROSTITUTES, DRUNKS AND DRUG ADDICTS ASKED ME FOR MONEY AS I SLOWLY WALKED THROUGH THE FLICKERING LIGHTS OF THE STALE SMELLY HALLWAY.

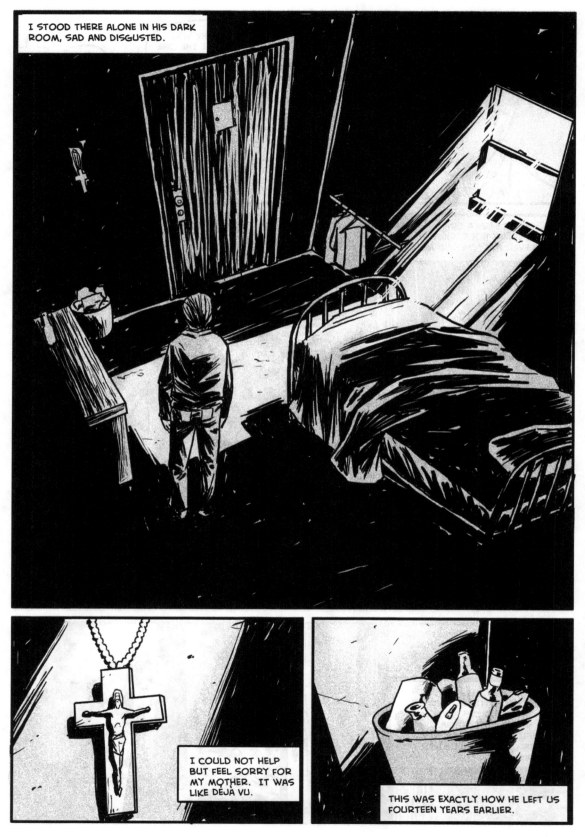

I STOOD THERE ALONE IN HIS DARK ROOM, SAD AND DISGUSTED.

I COULD NOT HELP BUT FEEL SORRY FOR MY MOTHER. IT WAS LIKE DÉJÀ VU.

THIS WAS EXACTLY HOW HE LEFT US FOURTEEN YEARS EARLIER.

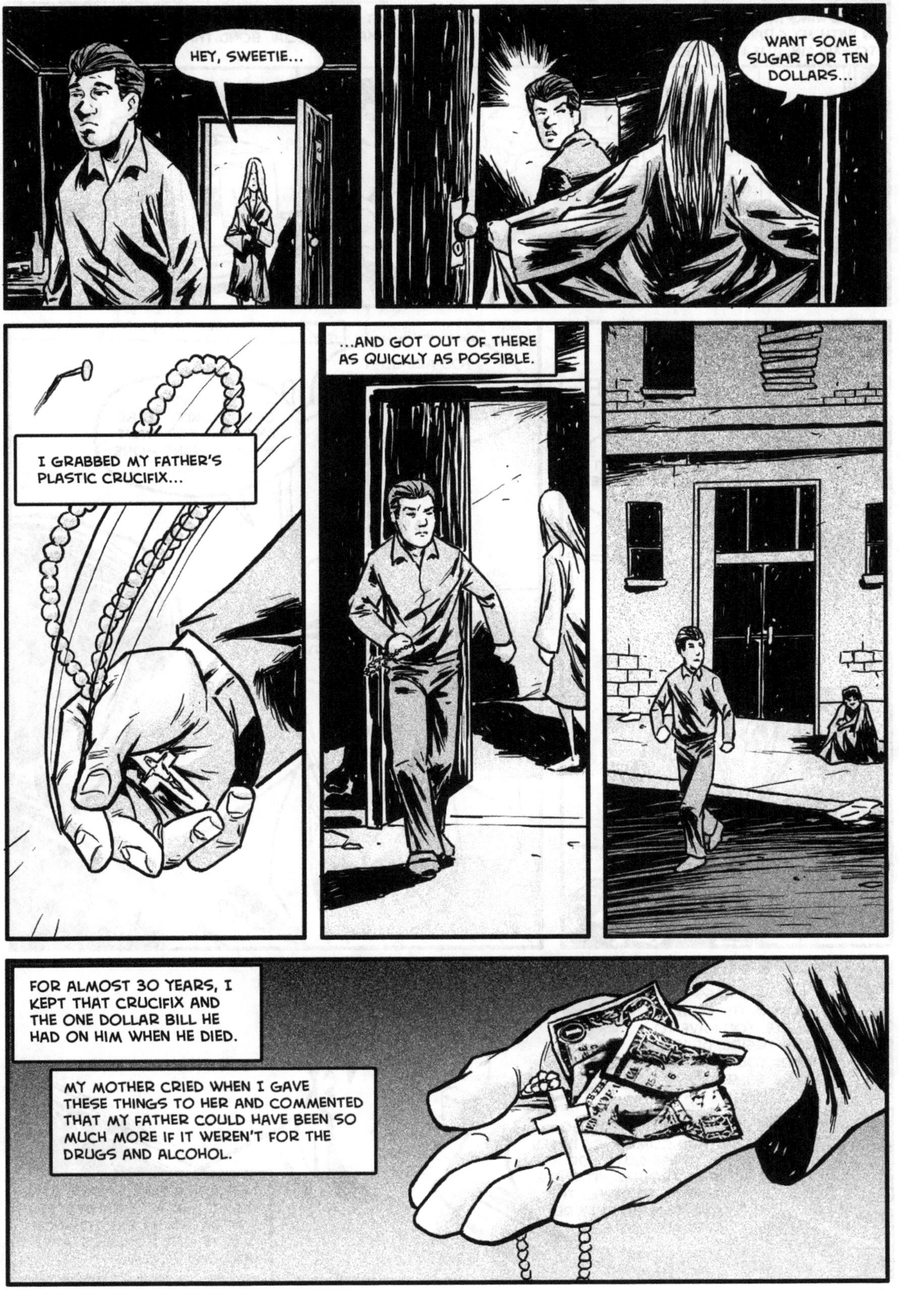
HEY, SWEETIE...
WANT SOME SUGAR FOR TEN DOLLARS...
I GRABBED MY FATHER'S PLASTIC CRUCIFIX...
...AND GOT OUT OF THERE AS QUICKLY AS POSSIBLE.
FOR ALMOST 30 YEARS, I KEPT THAT CRUCIFIX AND THE ONE DOLLAR BILL HE HAD ON HIM WHEN HE DIED.
MY MOTHER CRIED WHEN I GAVE THESE THINGS TO HER AND COMMENTED THAT MY FATHER COULD HAVE BEEN SO MUCH MORE IF IT WEREN'T FOR THE DRUGS AND ALCOHOL.

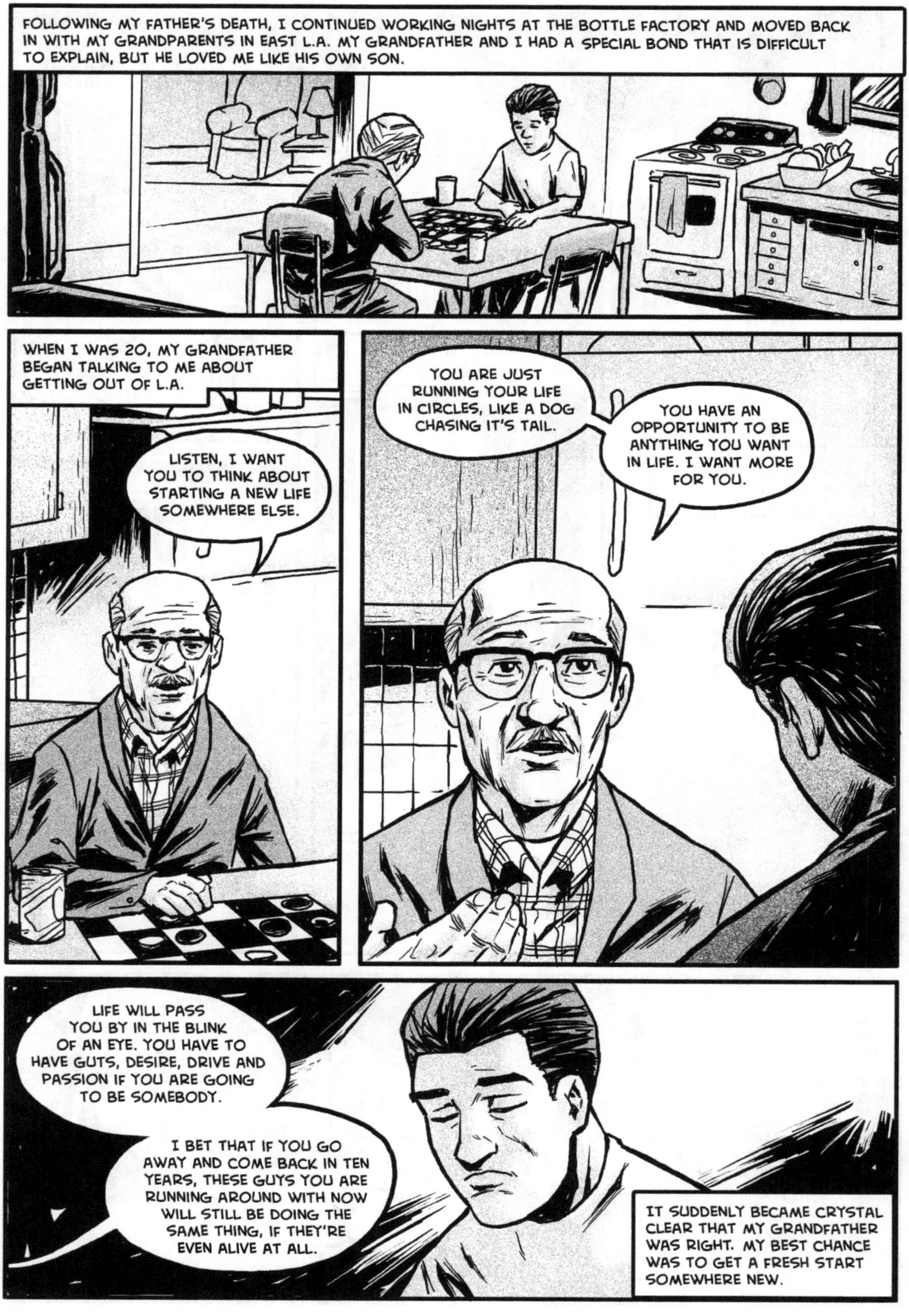
FOLLOWING MY FATHER'S DEATH, I CONTINUED WORKING NIGHTS AT THE BOTTLE FACTORY AND MOVED BACK IN WITH MY GRANDPARENTS IN EAST L.A. MY GRANDFATHER AND I HAD A SPECIAL BOND THAT IS DIFFICULT TO EXPLAIN, BUT HE LOVED ME LIKE HIS OWN SON.
WHEN I WAS 20, MY GRANDFATHER BEGAN TALKING TO ME ABOUT GETTING OUT OF L.A.
LISTEN, I WANT YOU TO THINK ABOUT STARTING A NEW LIFE SOMEWHERE ELSE.
YOU ARE JUST RUNNING YOUR LIFE IN CIRCLES, LIKE A DOG CHASING IT'S TAIL.
YOU HAVE AN OPPORTUNITY TO BE ANYTHING YOU WANT IN LIFE. I WANT MORE FOR YOU.
LIFE WILL PASS YOU BY IN THE BLINK OF AN EYE. YOU HAVE TO HAVE GUTS, DESIRE, DRIVE AND PASSION IF YOU ARE GOING TO BE SOMEBODY.
I BET THAT IF YOU GO AWAY AND COME BACK IN TEN YEARS, THESE GUYS YOU ARE RUNNING AROUND WITH NOW WILL STILL BE DOING THE SAME THING, IF THEY'RE EVEN ALIVE AT ALL.
IT SUDDENLY BECAME CRYSTAL CLEAR THAT MY GRANDFATHER WAS RIGHT. MY BEST CHANCE WAS TO GET A FRESH START SOMEWHERE NEW.

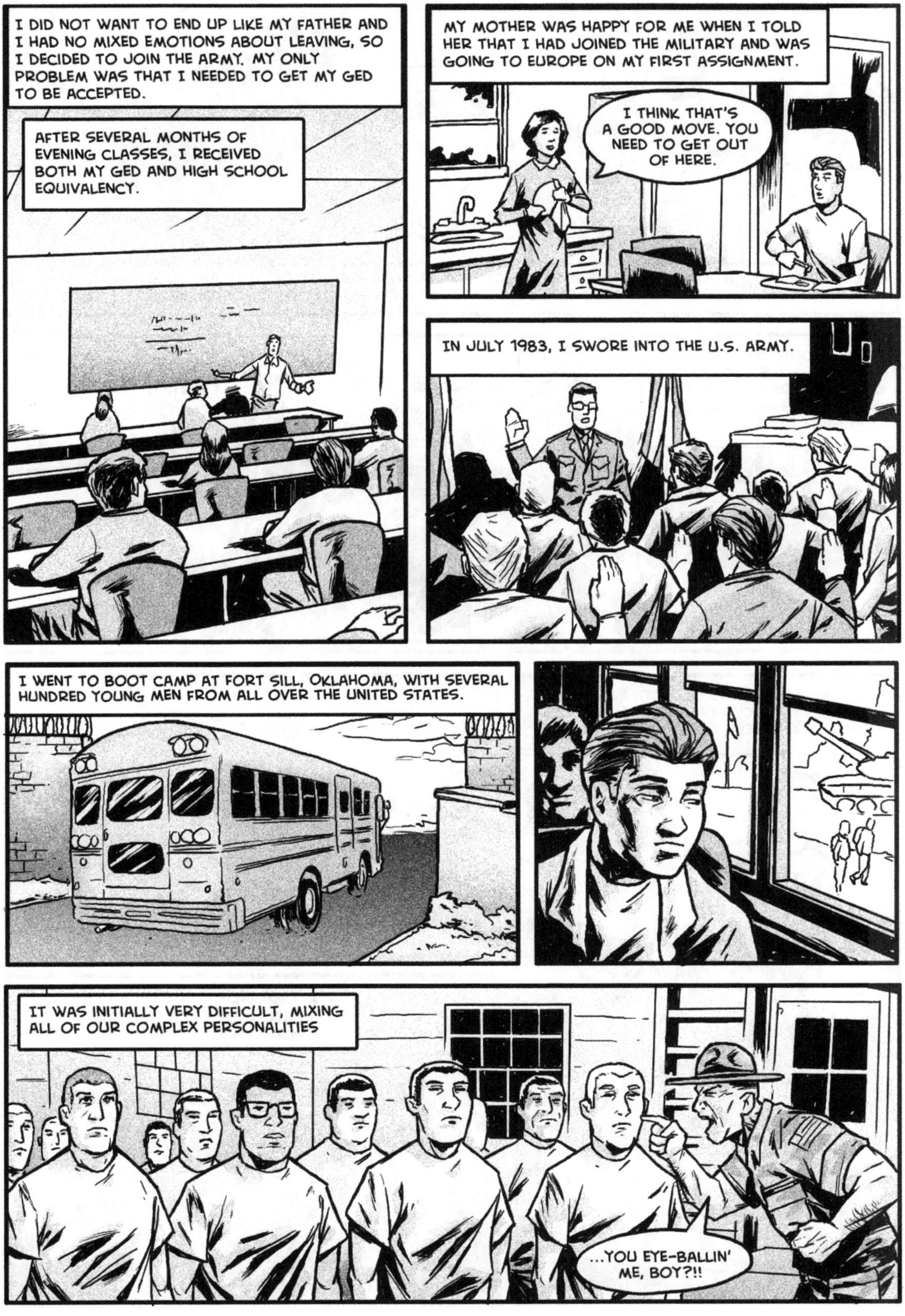
I DID NOT WANT TO END UP LIKE MY FATHER AND I HAD NO MIXED EMOTIONS ABOUT LEAVING, SO I DECIDED TO JOIN THE ARMY. MY ONLY PROBLEM WAS THAT I NEEDED TO GET MY GED TO BE ACCEPTED.
AFTER SEVERAL MONTHS OF EVENING CLASSES, I RECEIVED BOTH MY GED AND HIGH SCHOOL EQUIVALENCY.
MY MOTHER WAS HAPPY FOR ME WHEN I TOLD HER THAT I HAD JOINED THE MILITARY AND WAS GOING TO EUROPE ON MY FIRST ASSIGNMENT.
I THINK THAT'S A GOOD MOVE. YOU NEED TO GET OUT OF HERE.
IN JULY 1983, I SWORE INTO THE U.S. ARMY.
I WENT TO BOOT CAMP AT FORT SILL, OKLAHOMA, WITH SEVERAL HUNDRED YOUNG MEN FROM ALL OVER THE UNITED STATES.
IT WAS INITIALLY VERY DIFFICULT, MIXING ALL OF OUR COMPLEX PERSONALITIES
...YOU EYE-BALLIN' ME, BOY?!!

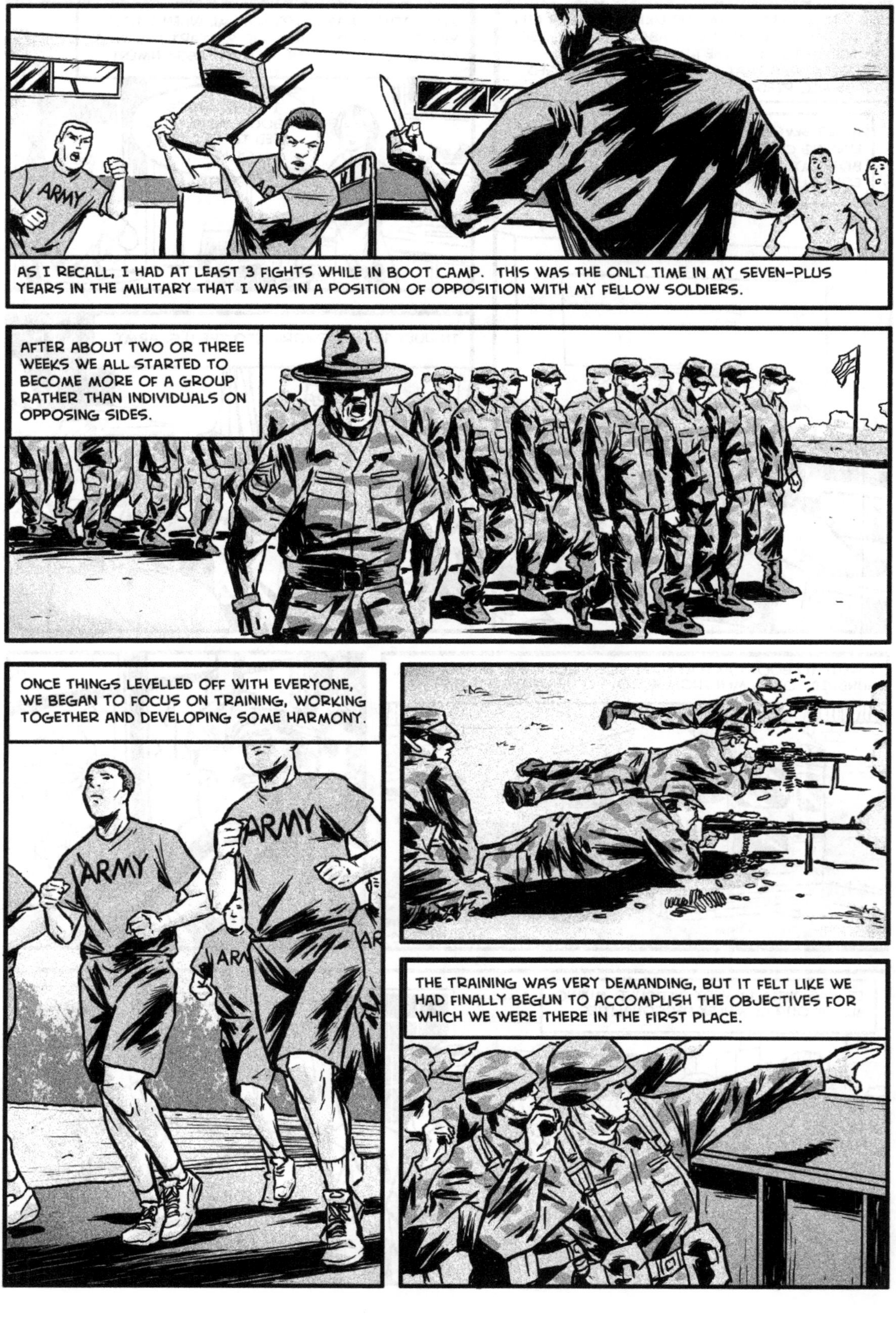
AS I RECALL, I HAD AT LEAST 3 FIGHTS WHILE IN BOOT CAMP. THIS WAS THE ONLY TIME IN MY SEVEN-PLUS YEARS IN THE MILITARY THAT I WAS IN A POSITION OF OPPOSITION WITH MY FELLOW SOLDIERS.
ARMY
AFTER ABOUT TWO OR THREE WEEKS WE ALL STARTED TO BECOME MORE OF A GROUP RATHER THAN INDIVIDUALS ON OPPOSING SIDES.
ONCE THINGS LEVELLED OFF WITH EVERYONE, WE BEGAN TO FOCUS ON TRAINING, WORKING TOGETHER AND DEVELOPING SOME HARMONY.
ARMY
ARMY
THE TRAINING WAS VERY DEMANDING, BUT IT FELT LIKE WE HAD FINALLY BEGUN TO ACCOMPLISH THE OBJECTIVES FOR WHICH WE WERE THERE IN THE FIRST PLACE.

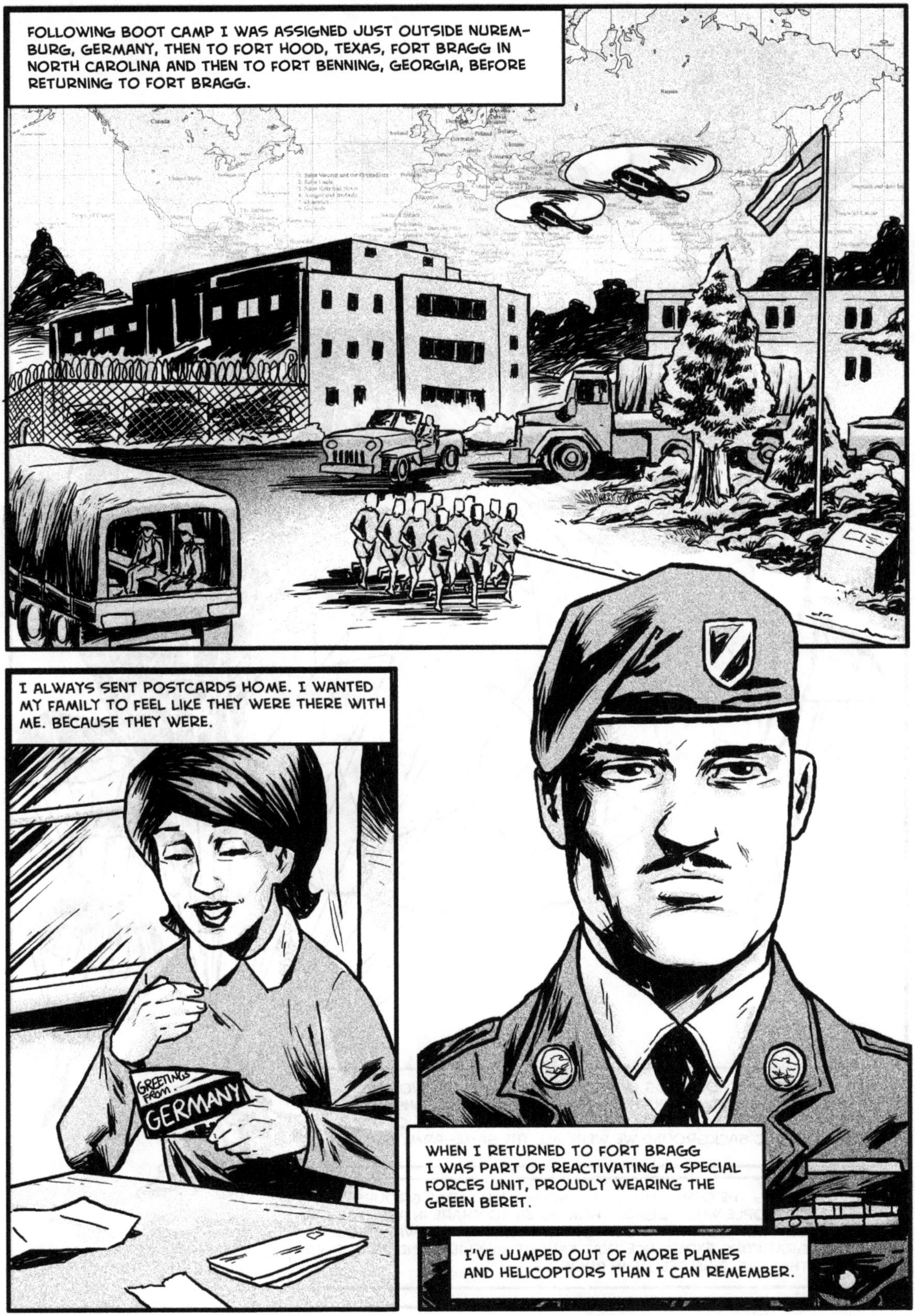
FOLLOWING BOOT CAMP I WAS ASSIGNED JUST OUTSIDE NUREMBURG, GERMANY, THEN TO FORT HOOD, TEXAS, FORT BRAGG IN NORTH CAROLINA AND THEN TO FORT BENNING, GEORGIA, BEFORE RETURNING TO FORT BRAGG.
I ALWAYS SENT POSTCARDS HOME. I WANTED MY FAMILY TO FEEL LIKE THEY WERE THERE WITH ME. BECAUSE THEY WERE.
GREETINGS FROM
GERMANY
WHEN I RETURNED TO FORT BRAGG I WAS PART OF REACTIVATING A SPECIAL FORCES UNIT, PROUDLY WEARING THE GREEN BERET.
I'VE JUMPED OUT OF MORE PLANES AND HELICOPTORS THAN I CAN REMEMBER.

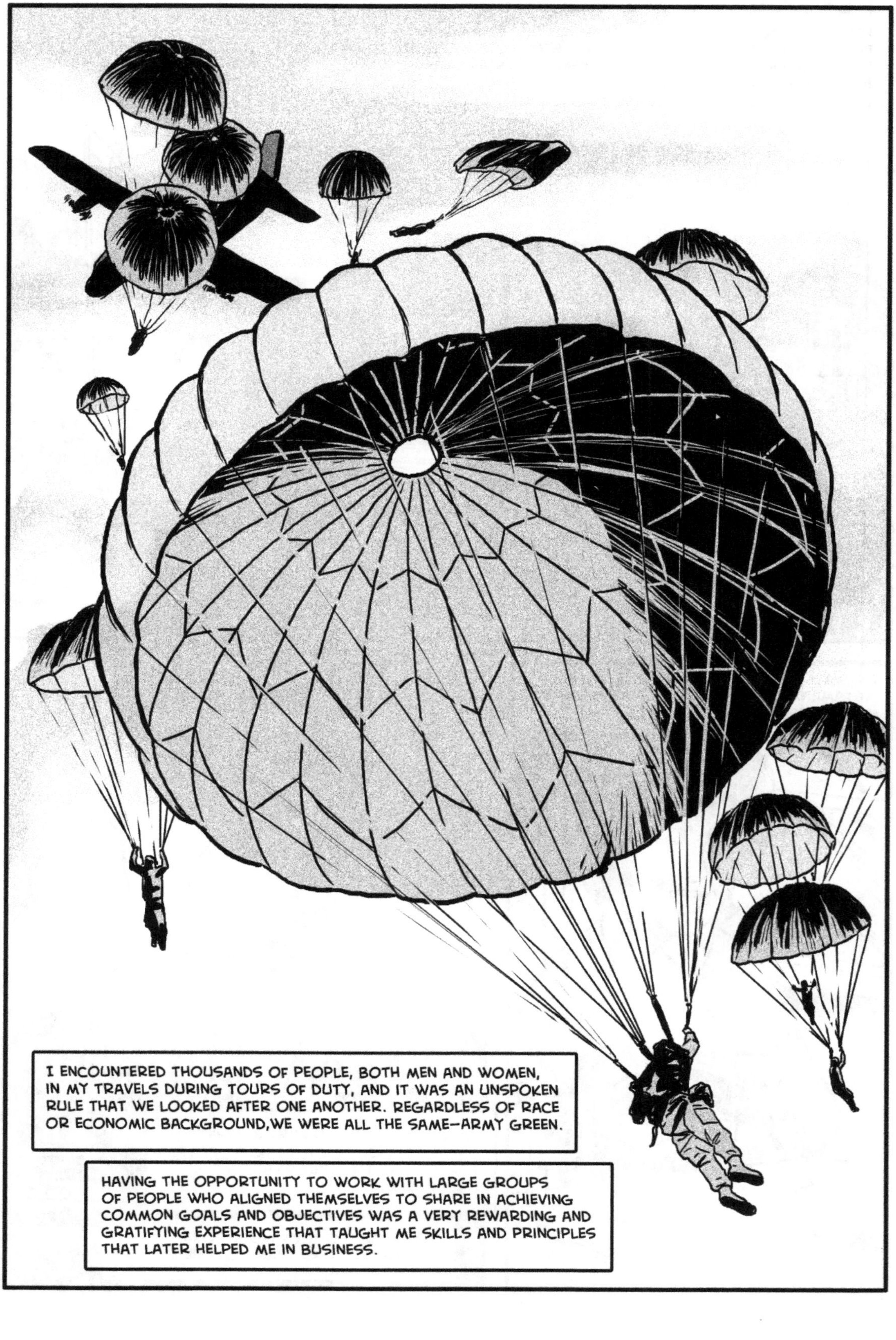
I ENCOUNTERED THOUSANDS OF PEOPLE, BOTH MEN AND WOMEN, IN MY TRAVELS DURING TOURS OF DUTY, AND IT WAS AN UNSPOKEN RULE THAT WE LOOKED AFTER ONE ANOTHER. REGARDLESS OF RACE OR ECONOMIC BACKGROUND, WE WERE ALL THE SAME—ARMY GREEN.
HAVING THE OPPORTUNITY TO WORK WITH LARGE GROUPS OF PEOPLE WHO ALIGNED THEMSELVES TO SHARE IN ACHIEVING COMMON GOALS AND OBJECTIVES WAS A VERY REWARDING AND GRATIFYING EXPERIENCE THAT TAUGHT ME SKILLS AND PRINCIPLES THAT LATER HELPED ME IN BUSINESS.

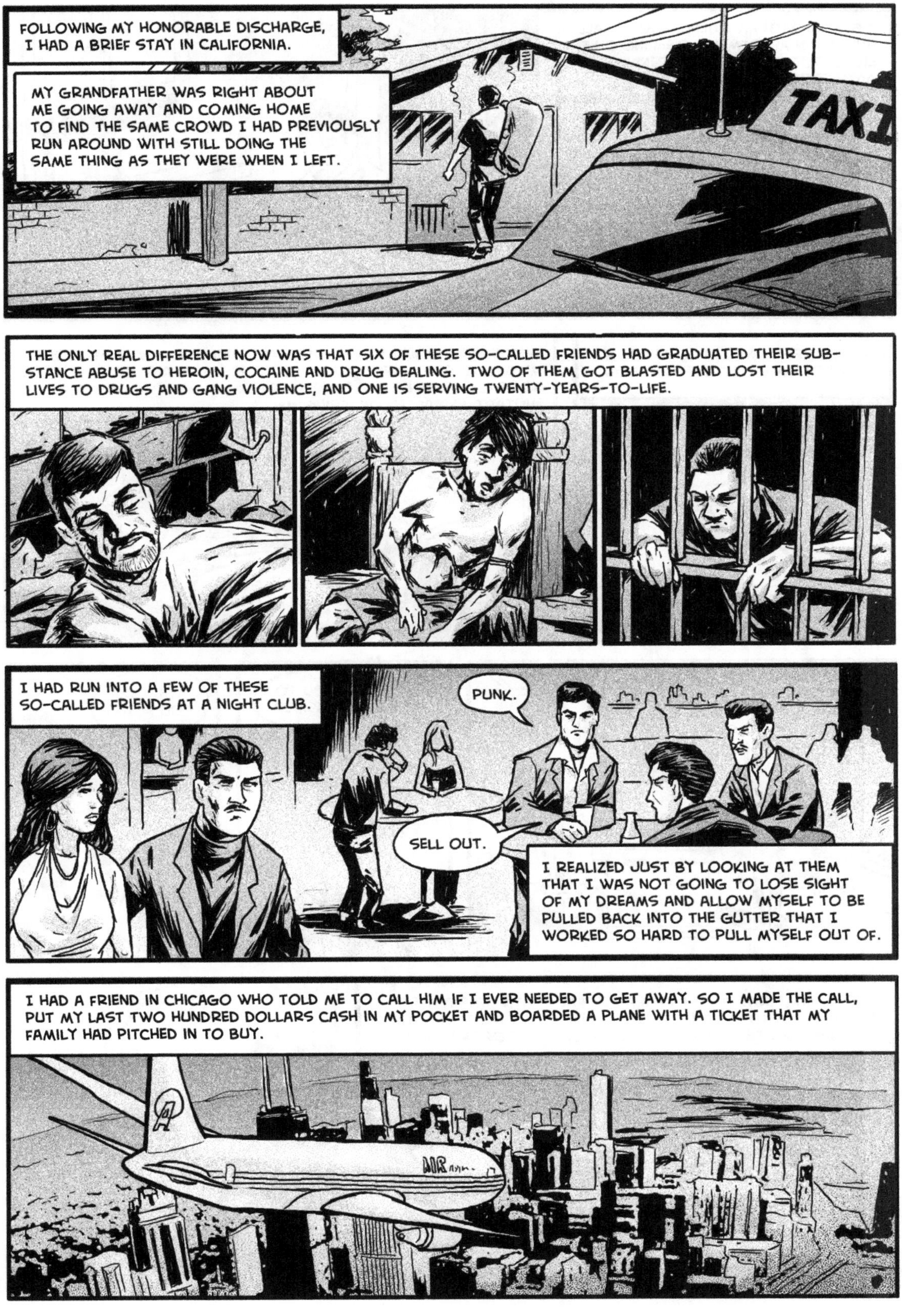

FOLLOWING MY HONORABLE DISCHARGE, I HAD A BRIEF STAY IN CALIFORNIA.
MY GRANDFATHER WAS RIGHT ABOUT ME GOING AWAY AND COMING HOME TO FIND THE SAME CROWD I HAD PREVIOUSLY RUN AROUND WITH STILL DOING THE SAME THING AS THEY WERE WHEN I LEFT.
TAXI
THE ONLY REAL DIFFERENCE NOW WAS THAT SIX OF THESE SO-CALLED FRIENDS HAD GRADUATED THEIR SUB-STANCE ABUSE TO HEROIN, COCAINE AND DRUG DEALING. TWO OF THEM GOT BLASTED AND LOST THEIR LIVES TO DRUGS AND GANG VIOLENCE, AND ONE IS SERVING TWENTY-YEARS-TO-LIFE.
I HAD RUN INTO A FEW OF THESE SO-CALLED FRIENDS AT A NIGHT CLUB.
PUNK.
SELL OUT.
I REALIZED JUST BY LOOKING AT THEM THAT I WAS NOT GOING TO LOSE SIGHT OF MY DREAMS AND ALLOW MYSELF TO BE PULLED BACK INTO THE GUTTER THAT I WORKED SO HARD TO PULL MYSELF OUT OF.
I HAD A FRIEND IN CHICAGO WHO TOLD ME TO CALL HIM IF I EVER NEEDED TO GET AWAY. SO I MADE THE CALL, PUT MY LAST TWO HUNDRED DOLLARS CASH IN MY POCKET AND BOARDED A PLANE WITH A TICKET THAT MY FAMILY HAD PITCHED IN TO BUY.

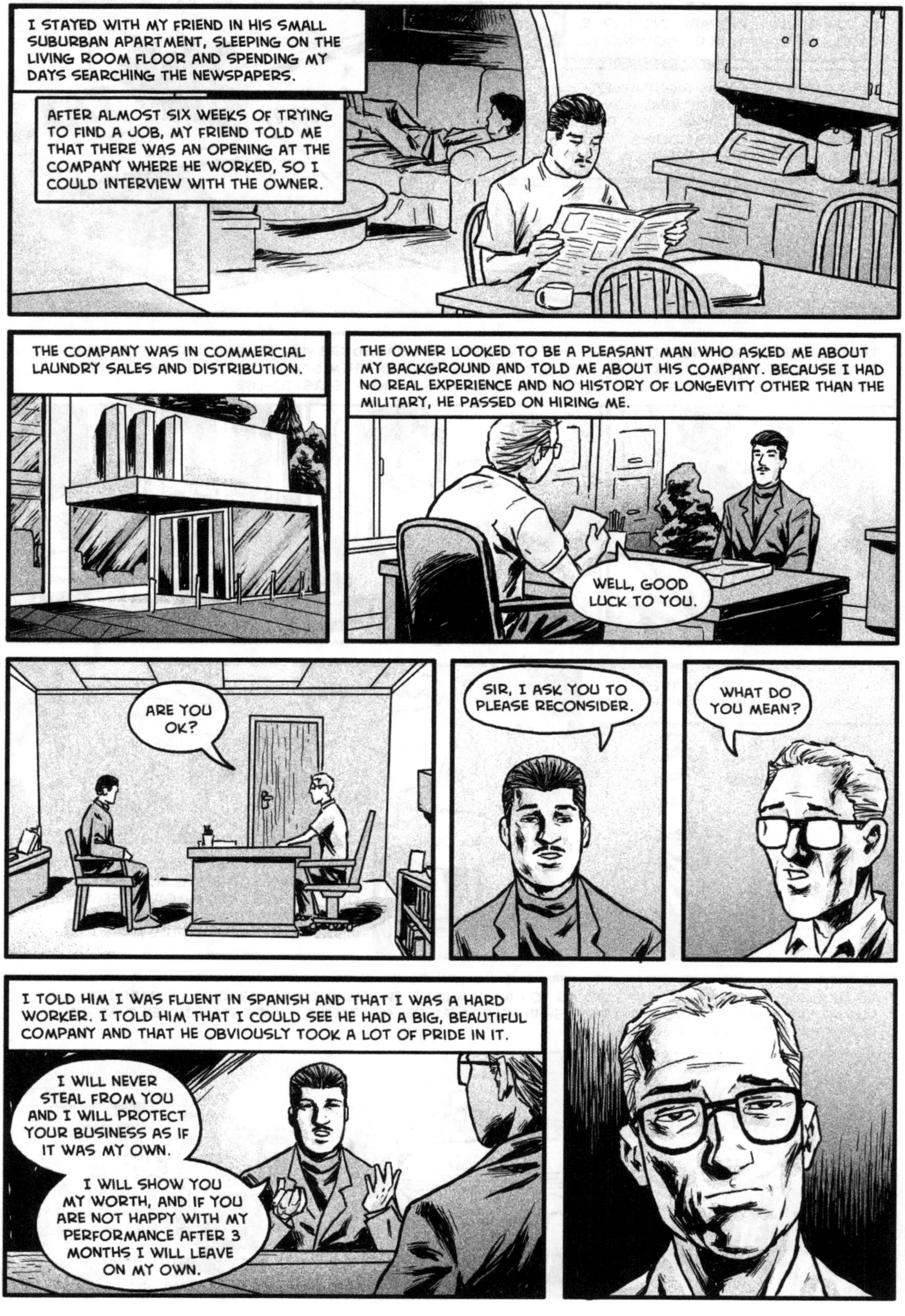
I STAYED WITH MY FRIEND IN HIS SMALL SUBURBAN APARTMENT, SLEEPING ON THE LIVING ROOM FLOOR AND SPENDING MY DAYS SEARCHING THE NEWSPAPERS.
AFTER ALMOST SIX WEEKS OF TRYING TO FIND A JOB, MY FRIEND TOLD ME THAT THERE WAS AN OPENING AT THE COMPANY WHERE HE WORKED, SO I COULD INTERVIEW WITH THE OWNER.
THE COMPANY WAS IN COMMERCIAL LAUNDRY SALES AND DISTRIBUTION.
THE OWNER LOOKED TO BE A PLEASANT MAN WHO ASKED ME ABOUT MY BACKGROUND AND TOLD ME ABOUT HIS COMPANY. BECAUSE I HAD NO REAL EXPERIENCE AND NO HISTORY OF LONGEVITY OTHER THAN THE MILITARY, HE PASSED ON HIRING ME.
WELL, GOOD LUCK TO YOU.
ARE YOU OK?
SIR, I ASK YOU TO PLEASE RECONSIDER.
WHAT DO YOU MEAN?
I TOLD HIM I WAS FLUENT IN SPANISH AND THAT I WAS A HARD WORKER. I TOLD HIM THAT I COULD SEE HE HAD A BIG, BEAUTIFUL COMPANY AND THAT HE OBVIOUSLY TOOK A LOT OF PRIDE IN IT.
I WILL NEVER STEAL FROM YOU AND I WILL PROTECT YOUR BUSINESS AS IF IT WAS MY OWN.
I WILL SHOW YOU MY WORTH, AND IF YOU ARE NOT HAPPY WITH MY PERFORMANCE AFTER 3 MONTHS I WILL LEAVE ON MY OWN.

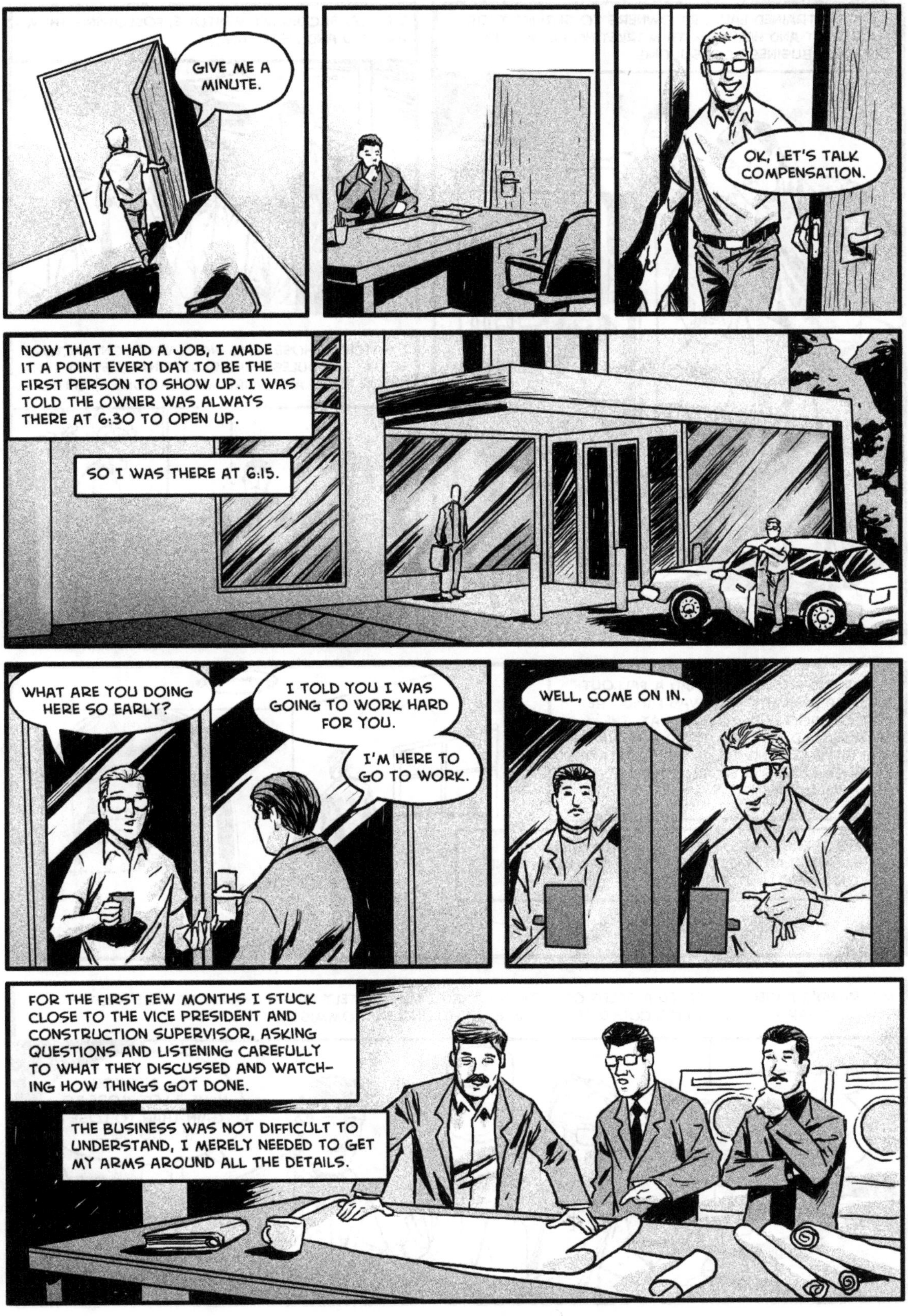
GIVE ME A MINUTE.
OK, LET'S TALK COMPENSATION.
NOW THAT I HAD A JOB, I MADE IT A POINT EVERY DAY TO BE THE FIRST PERSON TO SHOW UP. I WAS TOLD THE OWNER WAS ALWAYS THERE AT 6:30 TO OPEN UP.
SO I WAS THERE AT 6:15.
WHAT ARE YOU DOING HERE SO EARLY?
I TOLD YOU I WAS GOING TO WORK HARD FOR YOU.
I'M HERE TO GO TO WORK.
WELL, COME ON IN.
FOR THE FIRST FEW MONTHS I STUCK CLOSE TO THE VICE PRESIDENT AND CONSTRUCTION SUPERVISOR, ASKING QUESTIONS AND LISTENING CAREFULLY TO WHAT THEY DISCUSSED AND WATCH-ING HOW THINGS GOT DONE.
THE BUSINESS WAS NOT DIFFICULT TO UNDERSTAND, I MERELY NEEDED TO GET MY ARMS AROUND ALL THE DETAILS.

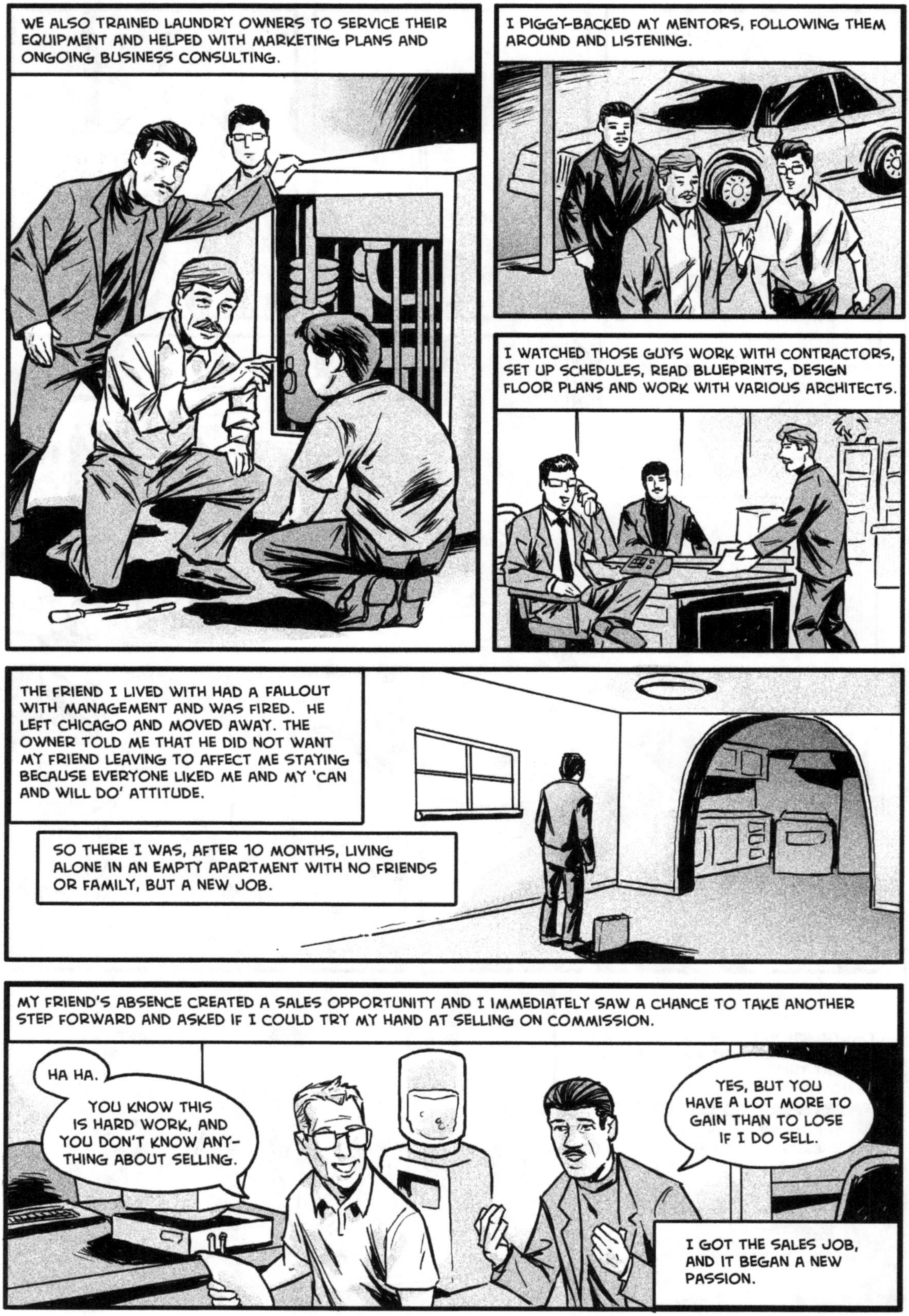
WE ALSO TRAINED LAUNDRY OWNERS TO SERVICE THEIR EQUIPMENT AND HELPED WITH MARKETING PLANS AND ONGOING BUSINESS CONSULTING.
I PIGGY-BACKED MY MENTORS, FOLLOWING THEM AROUND AND LISTENING.
I WATCHED THOSE GUYS WORK WITH CONTRACTORS, SET UP SCHEDULES, READ BLUEPRINTS, DESIGN FLOOR PLANS AND WORK WITH VARIOUS ARCHITECTS.
THE FRIEND I LIVED WITH HAD A FALLOUT WITH MANAGEMENT AND WAS FIRED. HE LEFT CHICAGO AND MOVED AWAY. THE OWNER TOLD ME THAT HE DID NOT WANT MY FRIEND LEAVING TO AFFECT ME STAYING BECAUSE EVERYONE LIKED ME AND MY 'CAN AND WILL DO' ATTITUDE.
SO THERE I WAS, AFTER 10 MONTHS, LIVING ALONE IN AN EMPTY APARTMENT WITH NO FRIENDS OR FAMILY, BUT A NEW JOB.
MY FRIEND'S ABSENCE CREATED A SALES OPPORTUNITY AND I IMMEDIATELY SAW A CHANCE TO TAKE ANOTHER STEP FORWARD AND ASKED IF I COULD TRY MY HAND AT SELLING ON COMMISSION.
HA HA.
YOU KNOW THIS IS HARD WORK, AND YOU DON'T KNOW ANY-THING ABOUT SELLING.
YES, BUT YOU HAVE A LOT MORE TO GAIN THAN TO LOSE IF I DO SELL.
I GOT THE SALES JOB, AND IT BEGAN A NEW PASSION.

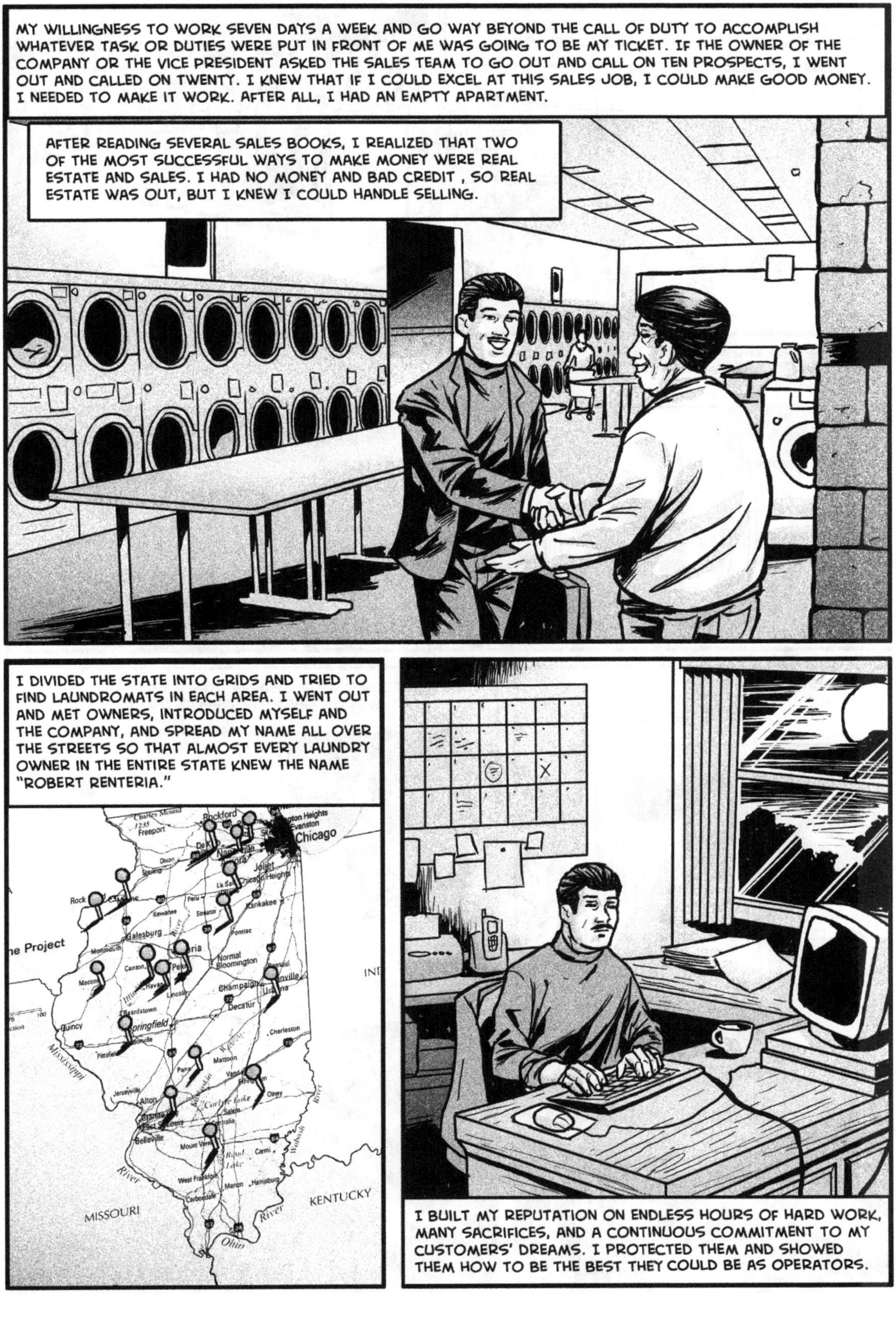
MY WILLINGNESS TO WORK SEVEN DAYS A WEEK AND GO WAY BEYOND THE CALL OF DUTY TO ACCOMPLISH WHATEVER TASK OR DUTIES WERE PUT IN FRONT OF ME WAS GOING TO BE MY TICKET. IF THE OWNER OF THE COMPANY OR THE VICE PRESIDENT ASKED THE SALES TEAM TO GO OUT AND CALL ON TEN PROSPECTS, I WENT OUT AND CALLED ON TWENTY. I KNEW THAT IF I COULD EXCEL AT THIS SALES JOB, I COULD MAKE GOOD MONEY. I NEEDED TO MAKE IT WORK. AFTER ALL, I HAD AN EMPTY APARTMENT.
AFTER READING SEVERAL SALES BOOKS, I REALIZED THAT TWO OF THE MOST SUCCESSFUL WAYS TO MAKE MONEY WERE REAL ESTATE AND SALES. I HAD NO MONEY AND BAD CREDIT , SO REAL ESTATE WAS OUT, BUT I KNEW I COULD HANDLE SELLING.
I DIVIDED THE STATE INTO GRIDS AND TRIED TO FIND LAUNDROMATS IN EACH AREA. I WENT OUT AND MET OWNERS, INTRODUCED MYSELF AND THE COMPANY, AND SPREAD MY NAME ALL OVER THE STREETS SO THAT ALMOST EVERY LAUNDRY OWNER IN THE ENTIRE STATE KNEW THE NAME "ROBERT RENTERIA."
Chicago
MISSOURI
KENTUCKY
I BUILT MY REPUTATION ON ENDLESS HOURS OF HARD WORK, MANY SACRIFICES, AND A CONTINUOUS COMMITMENT TO MY CUSTOMERS' DREAMS. I PROTECTED THEM AND SHOWED THEM HOW TO BE THE BEST THEY COULD BE AS OPERATORS.

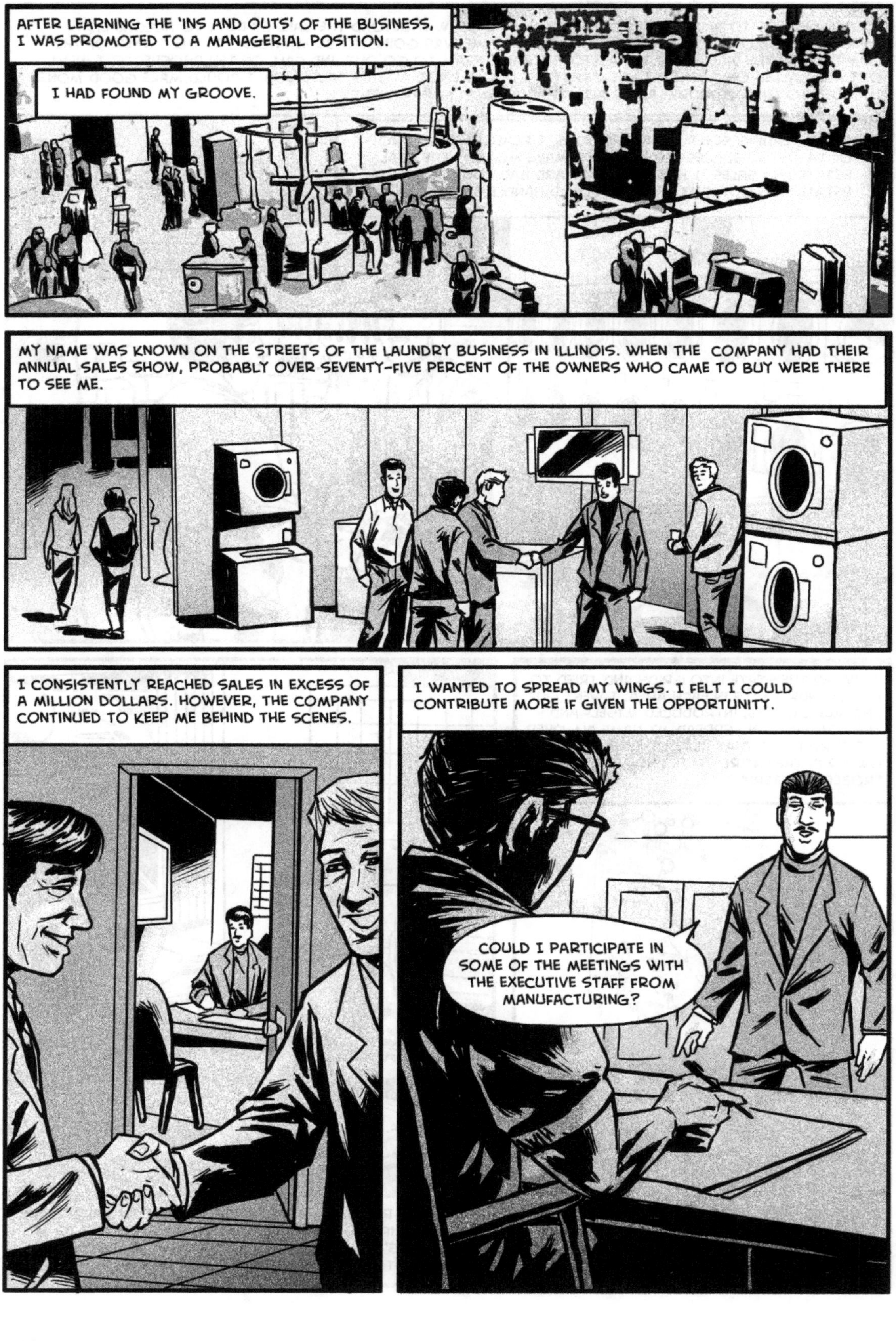
AFTER LEARNING THE 'INS AND OUTS' OF THE BUSINESS, I WAS PROMOTED TO A MANAGERIAL POSITION.
I HAD FOUND MY GROOVE.
MY NAME WAS KNOWN ON THE STREETS OF THE LAUNDRY BUSINESS IN ILLINOIS. WHEN THE COMPANY HAD THEIR ANNUAL SALES SHOW, PROBABLY OVER SEVENTY-FIVE PERCENT OF THE OWNERS WHO CAME TO BUY WERE THERE TO SEE ME.
I CONSISTENTLY REACHED SALES IN EXCESS OF A MILLION DOLLARS. HOWEVER, THE COMPANY CONTINUED TO KEEP ME BEHIND THE SCENES.
I WANTED TO SPREAD MY WINGS. I FELT I COULD CONTRIBUTE MORE IF GIVEN THE OPPORTUNITY.
COULD I PARTICIPATE IN SOME OF THE MEETINGS WITH THE EXECUTIVE STAFF FROM MANUFACTURING?

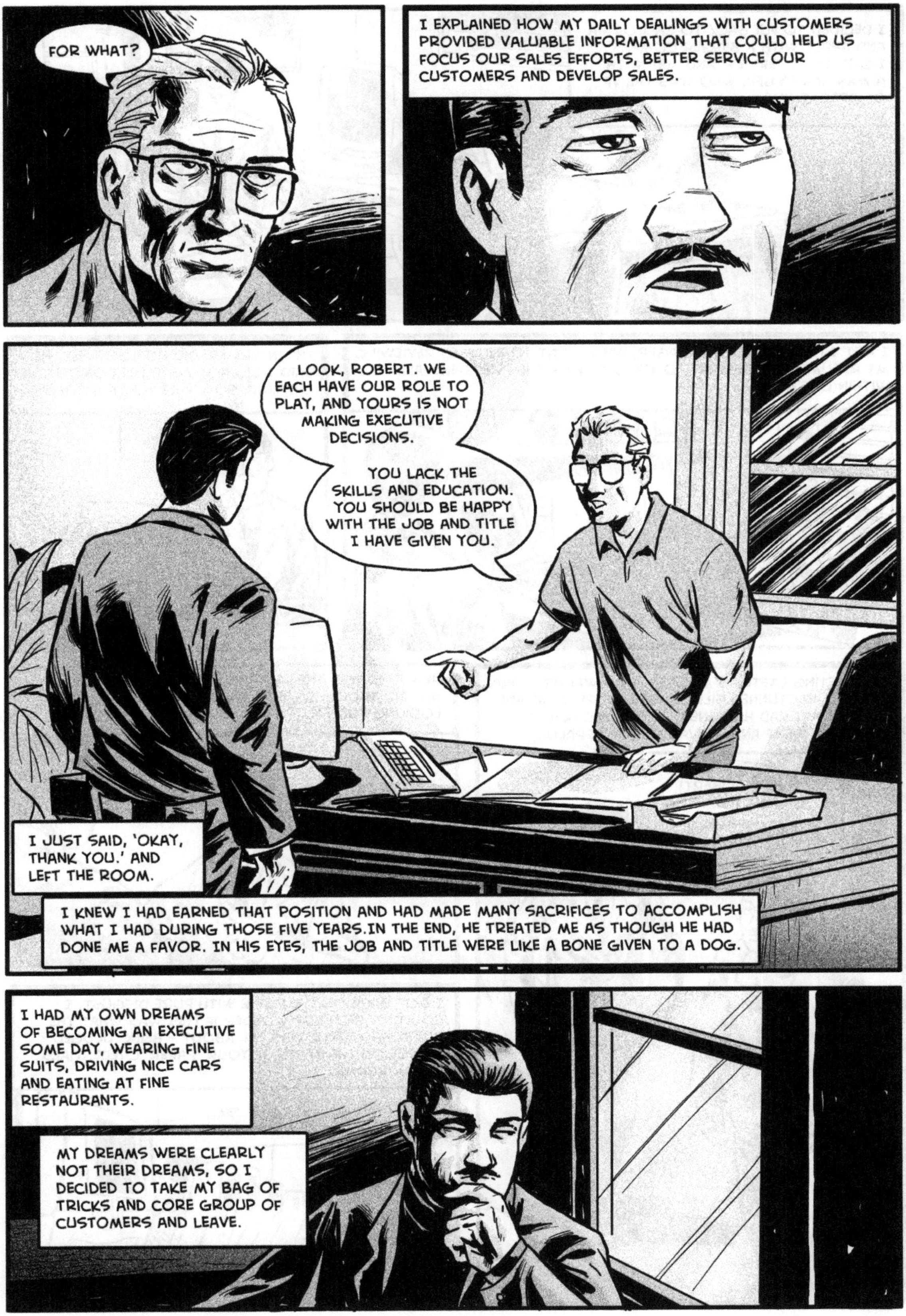
FOR WHAT?
I EXPLAINED HOW MY DAILY DEALINGS WITH CUSTOMERS PROVIDED VALUABLE INFORMATION THAT COULD HELP US FOCUS OUR SALES EFFORTS, BETTER SERVICE OUR CUSTOMERS AND DEVELOP SALES.
LOOK, ROBERT. WE EACH HAVE OUR ROLE TO PLAY, AND YOURS IS NOT MAKING EXECUTIVE DECISIONS.
YOU LACK THE SKILLS AND EDUCATION. YOU SHOULD BE HAPPY WITH THE JOB AND TITLE I HAVE GIVEN YOU.
I JUST SAID, 'OKAY, THANK YOU.' AND LEFT THE ROOM.
I KNEW I HAD EARNED THAT POSITION AND HAD MADE MANY SACRIFICES TO ACCOMPLISH WHAT I HAD DURING THOSE FIVE YEARS.IN THE END, HE TREATED ME AS THOUGH HE HAD DONE ME A FAVOR. IN HIS EYES, THE JOB AND TITLE WERE LIKE A BONE GIVEN TO A DOG.
I HAD MY OWN DREAMS OF BECOMING AN EXECUTIVE SOME DAY, WEARING FINE SUITS, DRIVING NICE CARS AND EATING AT FINE RESTAURANTS.
MY DREAMS WERE CLEARLY NOT THEIR DREAMS, SO I DECIDED TO TAKE MY BAG OF TRICKS AND CORE GROUP OF CUSTOMERS AND LEAVE.

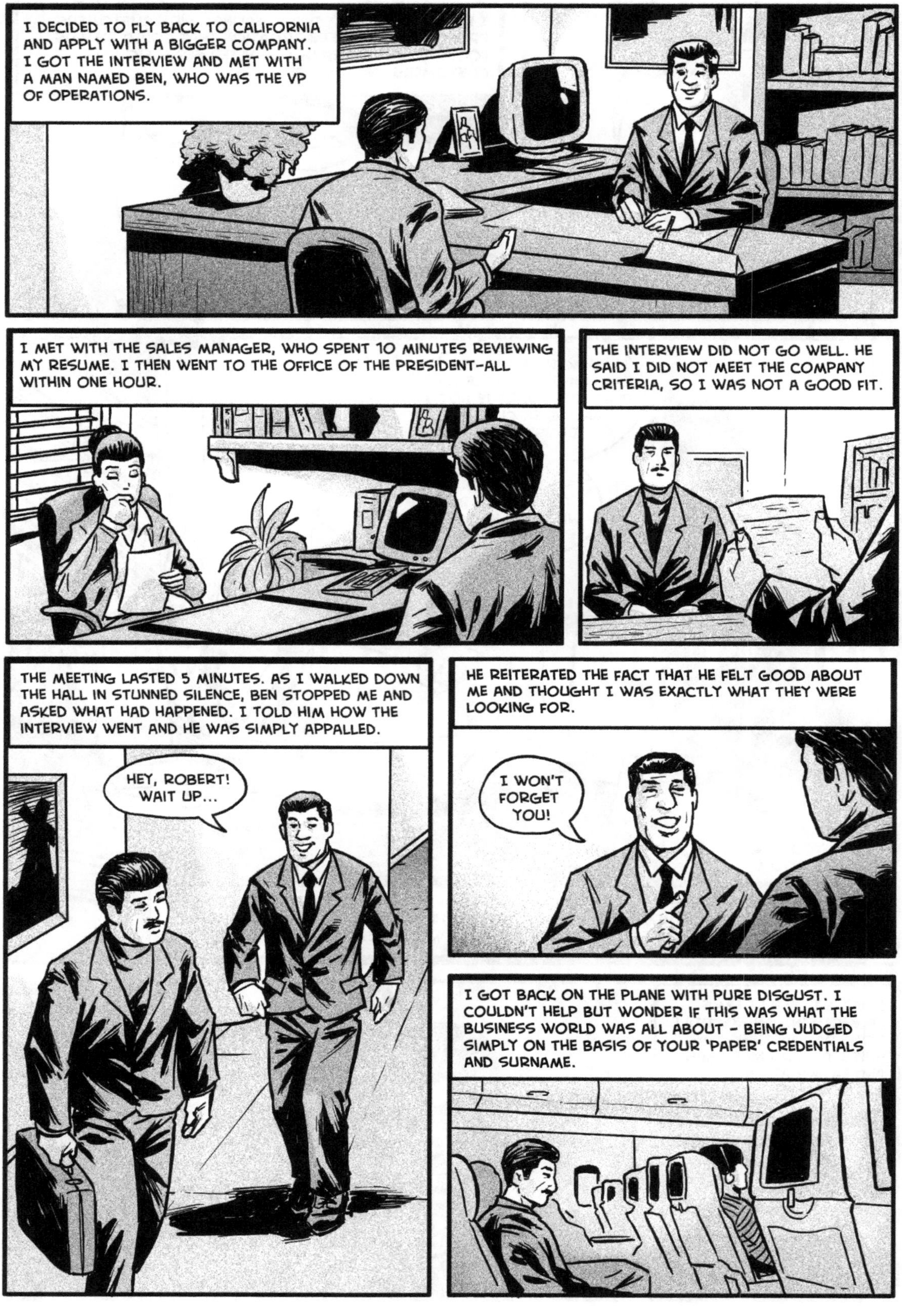
I DECIDED TO FLY BACK TO CALIFORNIA AND APPLY WITH A BIGGER COMPANY. I GOT THE INTERVIEW AND MET WITH A MAN NAMED BEN, WHO WAS THE VP OF OPERATIONS.
I MET WITH THE SALES MANAGER, WHO SPENT 10 MINUTES REVIEWING MY RESUME. I THEN WENT TO THE OFFICE OF THE PRESIDENT-ALL WITHIN ONE HOUR.
THE INTERVIEW DID NOT GO WELL. HE SAID I DID NOT MEET THE COMPANY CRITERIA, SO I WAS NOT A GOOD FIT.
THE MEETING LASTED 5 MINUTES. AS I WALKED DOWN THE HALL IN STUNNED SILENCE, BEN STOPPED ME AND ASKED WHAT HAD HAPPENED. I TOLD HIM HOW THE INTERVIEW WENT AND HE WAS SIMPLY APPALLED.
HEY, ROBERT! WAIT UP...
HE REITERATED THE FACT THAT HE FELT GOOD ABOUT ME AND THOUGHT I WAS EXACTLY WHAT THEY WERE LOOKING FOR.
I WON'T FORGET YOU!
I GOT BACK ON THE PLANE WITH PURE DISGUST. I COULDN'T HELP BUT WONDER IF THIS WAS WHAT THE BUSINESS WORLD WAS ALL ABOUT - BEING JUDGED SIMPLY ON THE BASIS OF YOUR 'PAPER' CREDENTIALS AND SURNAME.

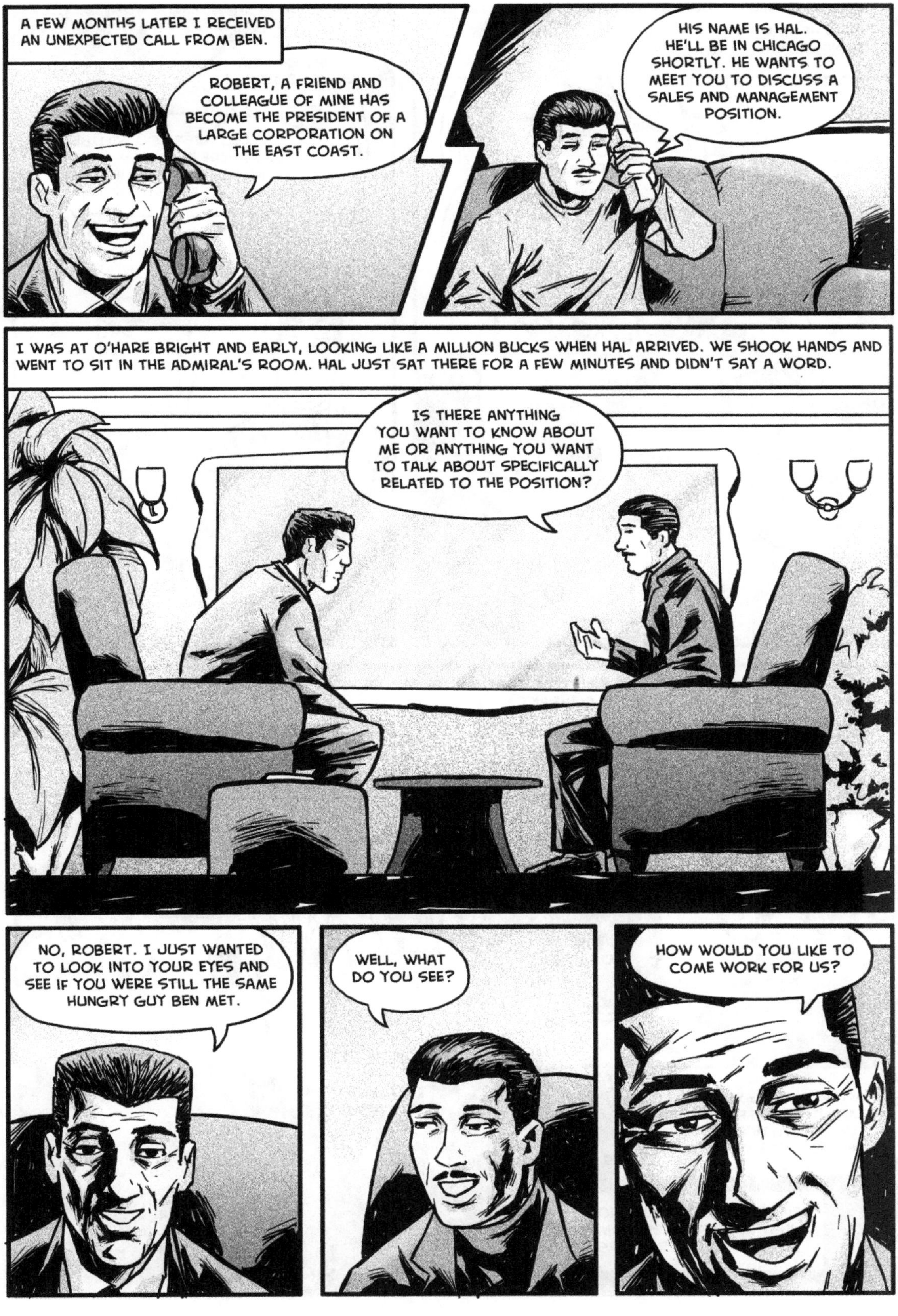
A FEW MONTHS LATER I RECEIVED AN UNEXPECTED CALL FROM BEN.
ROBERT, A FRIEND AND COLLEAGUE OF MINE HAS BECOME THE PRESIDENT OF A LARGE CORPORATION ON THE EAST COAST.
HIS NAME IS HAL. HE'LL BE IN CHICAGO SHORTLY. HE WANTS TO MEET YOU TO DISCUSS A SALES AND MANAGEMENT POSITION.
I WAS AT O'HARE BRIGHT AND EARLY, LOOKING LIKE A MILLION BUCKS WHEN HAL ARRIVED. WE SHOOK HANDS AND WENT TO SIT IN THE ADMIRAL'S ROOM. HAL JUST SAT THERE FOR A FEW MINUTES AND DIDN'T SAY A WORD.
IS THERE ANYTHING YOU WANT TO KNOW ABOUT ME OR ANYTHING YOU WANT TO TALK ABOUT SPECIFICALLY RELATED TO THE POSITION?
NO, ROBERT. I JUST WANTED TO LOOK INTO YOUR EYES AND SEE IF YOU WERE STILL THE SAME HUNGRY GUY BEN MET.
WELL, WHAT DO YOU SEE?
HOW WOULD YOU LIKE TO COME WORK FOR US?

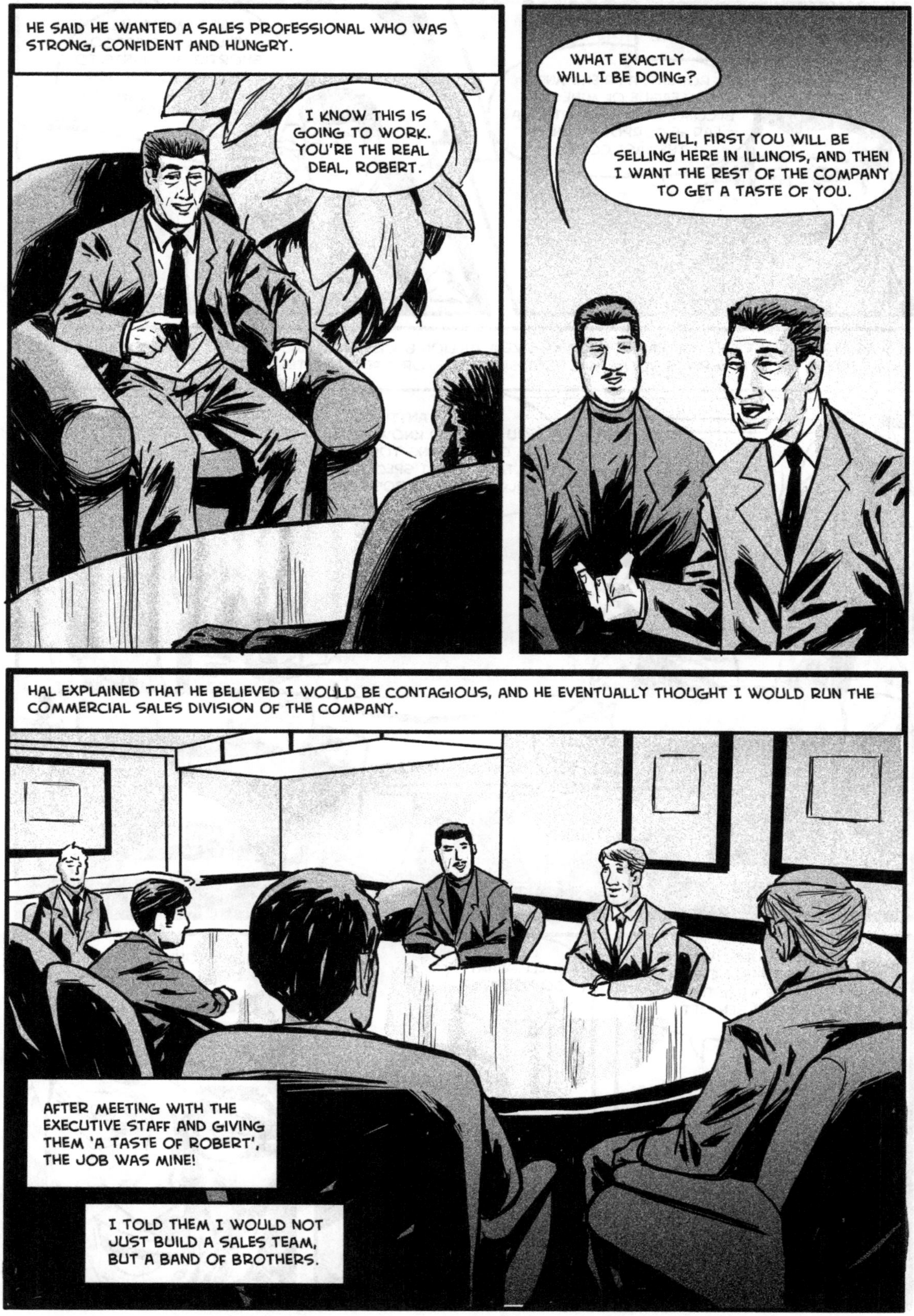
HE SAID HE WANTED A SALES PROFESSIONAL WHO WAS STRONG, CONFIDENT AND HUNGRY.
I KNOW THIS IS GOING TO WORK. YOU'RE THE REAL DEAL, ROBERT.
WHAT EXACTLY WILL I BE DOING?
WELL, FIRST YOU WILL BE SELLING HERE IN ILLINOIS, AND THEN I WANT THE REST OF THE COMPANY TO GET A TASTE OF YOU.
HAL EXPLAINED THAT HE BELIEVED I WOULD BE CONTAGIOUS, AND HE EVENTUALLY THOUGHT I WOULD RUN THE COMMERCIAL SALES DIVISION OF THE COMPANY.
AFTER MEETING WITH THE EXECUTIVE STAFF AND GIVING THEM 'A TASTE OF ROBERT', THE JOB WAS MINE!
I TOLD THEM I WOULD NOT JUST BUILD A SALES TEAM, BUT A BAND OF BROTHERS.

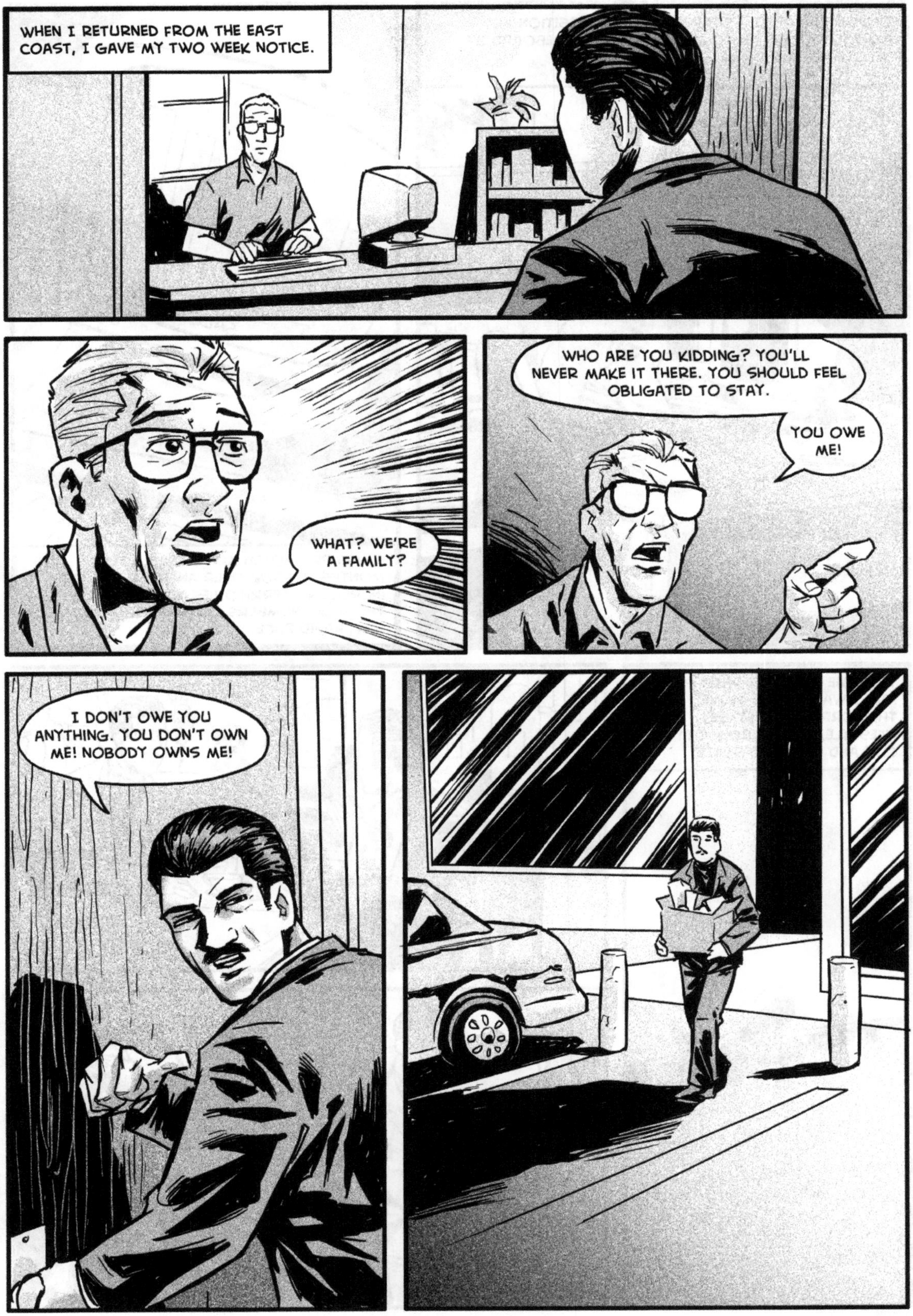
WHEN I RETURNED FROM THE EAST COAST, I GAVE MY TWO WEEK NOTICE.
WHAT? WE'RE A FAMILY?
WHO ARE YOU KIDDING? YOU'LL NEVER MAKE IT THERE. YOU SHOULD FEEL OBLIGATED TO STAY.
YOU OWE ME!
I DON'T OWE YOU ANYTHING. YOU DON'T OWN ME! NOBODY OWNS ME!

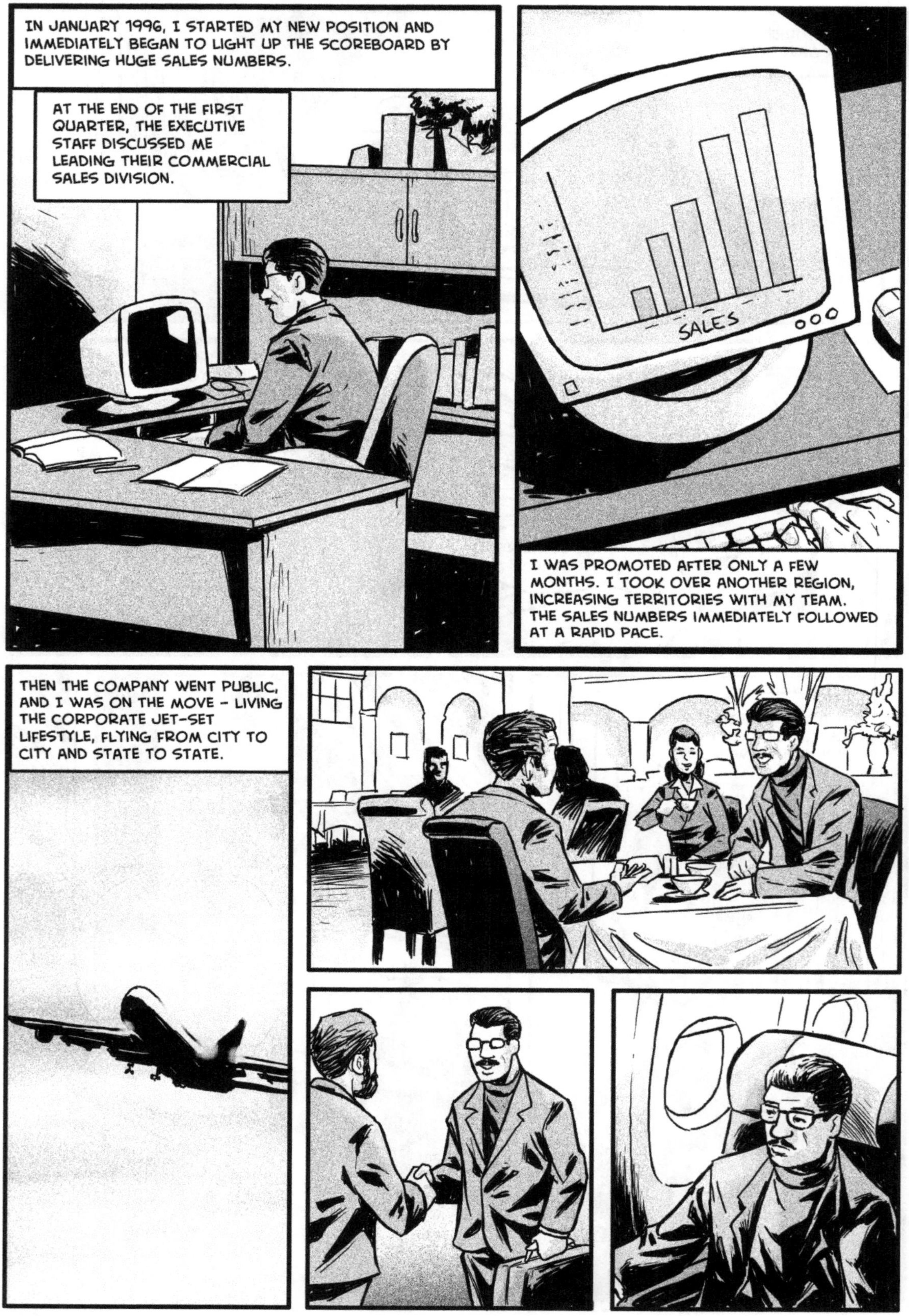
IN JANUARY 1996, I STARTED MY NEW POSITION AND IMMEDIATELY BEGAN TO LIGHT UP THE SCOREBOARD BY DELIVERING HUGE SALES NUMBERS.
AT THE END OF THE FIRST QUARTER, THE EXECUTIVE STAFF DISCUSSED ME LEADING THEIR COMMERCIAL SALES DIVISION.
SALES
I WAS PROMOTED AFTER ONLY A FEW MONTHS. I TOOK OVER ANOTHER REGION, INCREASING TERRITORIES WITH MY TEAM. THE SALES NUMBERS IMMEDIATELY FOLLOWED AT A RAPID PACE.
THEN THE COMPANY WENT PUBLIC, AND I WAS ON THE MOVE – LIVING THE CORPORATE JET-SET LIFESTYLE, FLYING FROM CITY TO CITY AND STATE TO STATE.

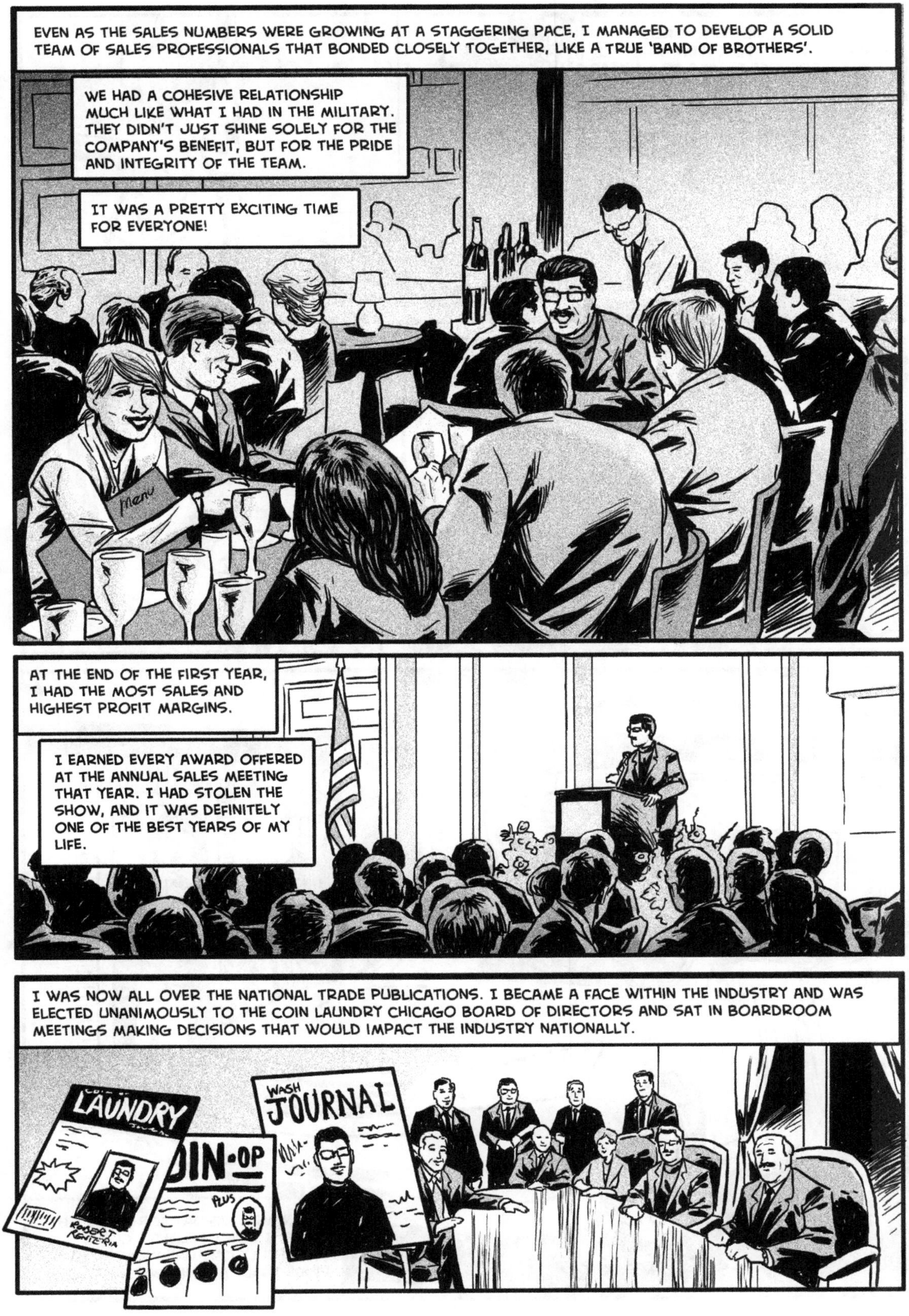
EVEN AS THE SALES NUMBERS WERE GROWING AT A STAGGERING PACE, I MANAGED TO DEVELOP A SOLID TEAM OF SALES PROFESSIONALS THAT BONDED CLOSELY TOGETHER, LIKE A TRUE 'BAND OF BROTHERS'.
WE HAD A COHESIVE RELATIONSHIP MUCH LIKE WHAT I HAD IN THE MILITARY. THEY DIDN'T JUST SHINE SOLELY FOR THE COMPANY'S BENEFIT, BUT FOR THE PRIDE AND INTEGRITY OF THE TEAM.
IT WAS A PRETTY EXCITING TIME FOR EVERYONE!
Menu
AT THE END OF THE FIRST YEAR, I HAD THE MOST SALES AND HIGHEST PROFIT MARGINS.
I EARNED EVERY AWARD OFFERED AT THE ANNUAL SALES MEETING THAT YEAR. I HAD STOLEN THE SHOW, AND IT WAS DEFINITELY ONE OF THE BEST YEARS OF MY LIFE.
I WAS NOW ALL OVER THE NATIONAL TRADE PUBLICATIONS. I BECAME A FACE WITHIN THE INDUSTRY AND WAS ELECTED UNANIMOUSLY TO THE COIN LAUNDRY CHICAGO BOARD OF DIRECTORS AND SAT IN BOARDROOM MEETINGS MAKING DECISIONS THAT WOULD IMPACT THE INDUSTRY NATIONALLY.
LAUNDRY
ROBERT RENTERIA
PLUS
WASH
JOURNAL

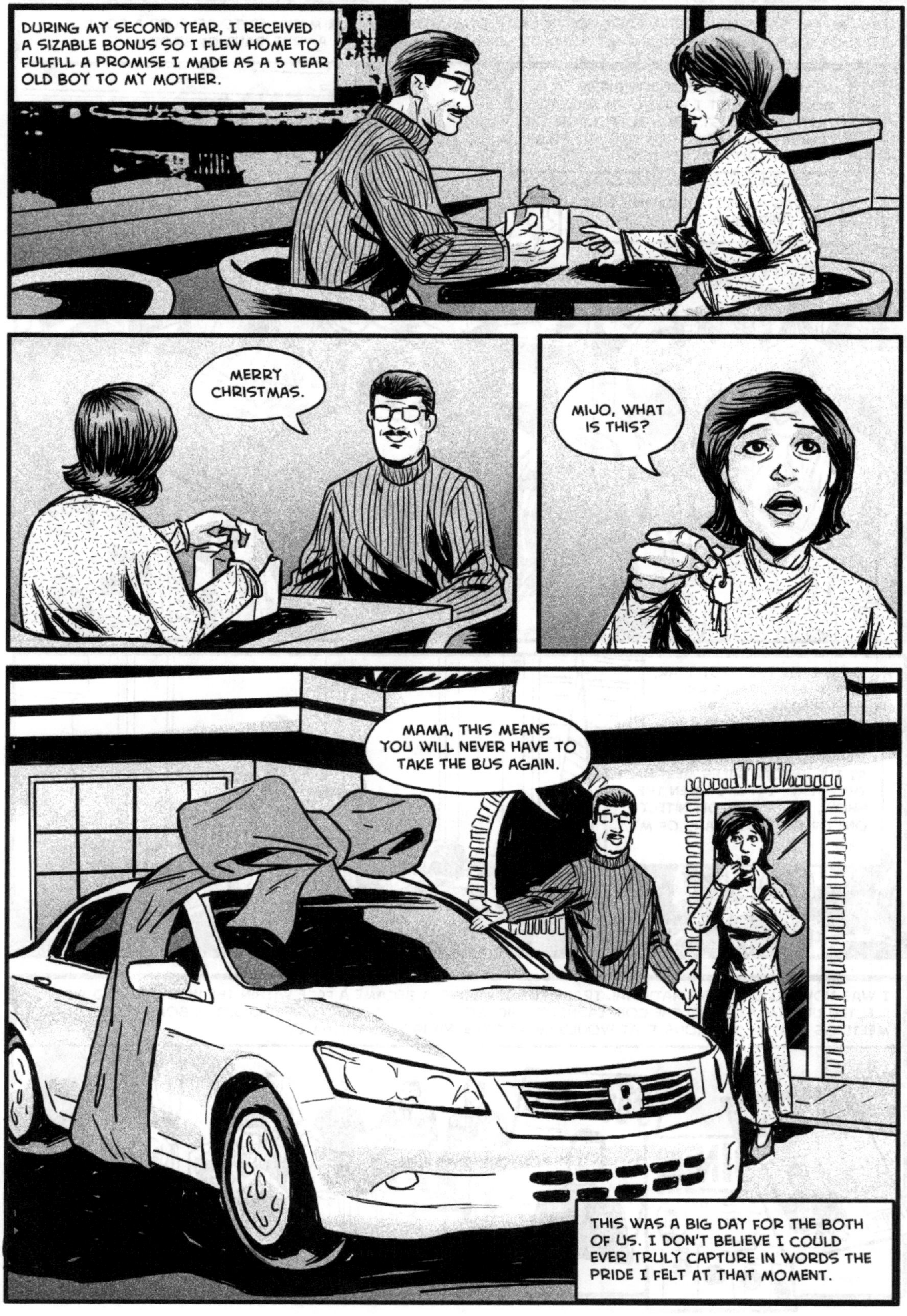
DURING MY SECOND YEAR, I RECEIVED A SIZABLE BONUS SO I FLEW HOME TO FULFILL A PROMISE I MADE AS A 5 YEAR OLD BOY TO MY MOTHER.
MERRY CHRISTMAS.
MIJO, WHAT IS THIS?
MAMA, THIS MEANS YOU WILL NEVER HAVE TO TAKE THE BUS AGAIN.
THIS WAS A BIG DAY FOR THE BOTH OF US. I DON'T BELIEVE I COULD EVER TRULY CAPTURE IN WORDS THE PRIDE I FELT AT THAT MOMENT.

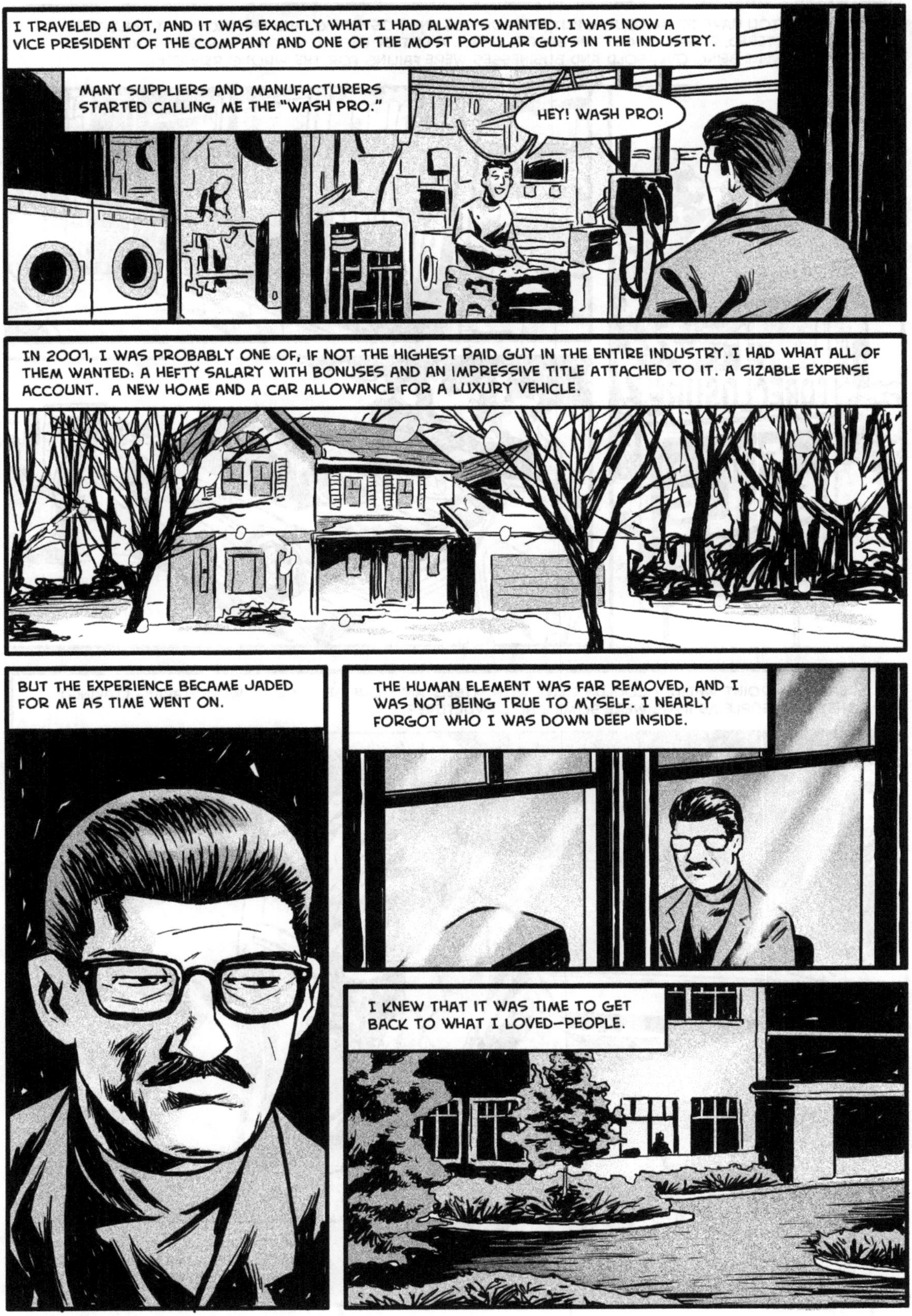
I TRAVELED A LOT, AND IT WAS EXACTLY WHAT I HAD ALWAYS WANTED. I WAS NOW A VICE PRESIDENT OF THE COMPANY AND ONE OF THE MOST POPULAR GUYS IN THE INDUSTRY.
MANY SUPPLIERS AND MANUFACTURERS STARTED CALLING ME THE "WASH PRO."
HEY! WASH PRO!
IN 2001, I WAS PROBABLY ONE OF, IF NOT THE HIGHEST PAID GUY IN THE ENTIRE INDUSTRY. I HAD WHAT ALL OF THEM WANTED: A HEFTY SALARY WITH BONUSES AND AN IMPRESSIVE TITLE ATTACHED TO IT. A SIZABLE EXPENSE ACCOUNT. A NEW HOME AND A CAR ALLOWANCE FOR A LUXURY VEHICLE.
BUT THE EXPERIENCE BECAME JADED FOR ME AS TIME WENT ON.
THE HUMAN ELEMENT WAS FAR REMOVED, AND I WAS NOT BEING TRUE TO MYSELF. I NEARLY FORGOT WHO I WAS DOWN DEEP INSIDE.
I KNEW THAT IT WAS TIME TO GET BACK TO WHAT I LOVED—PEOPLE.

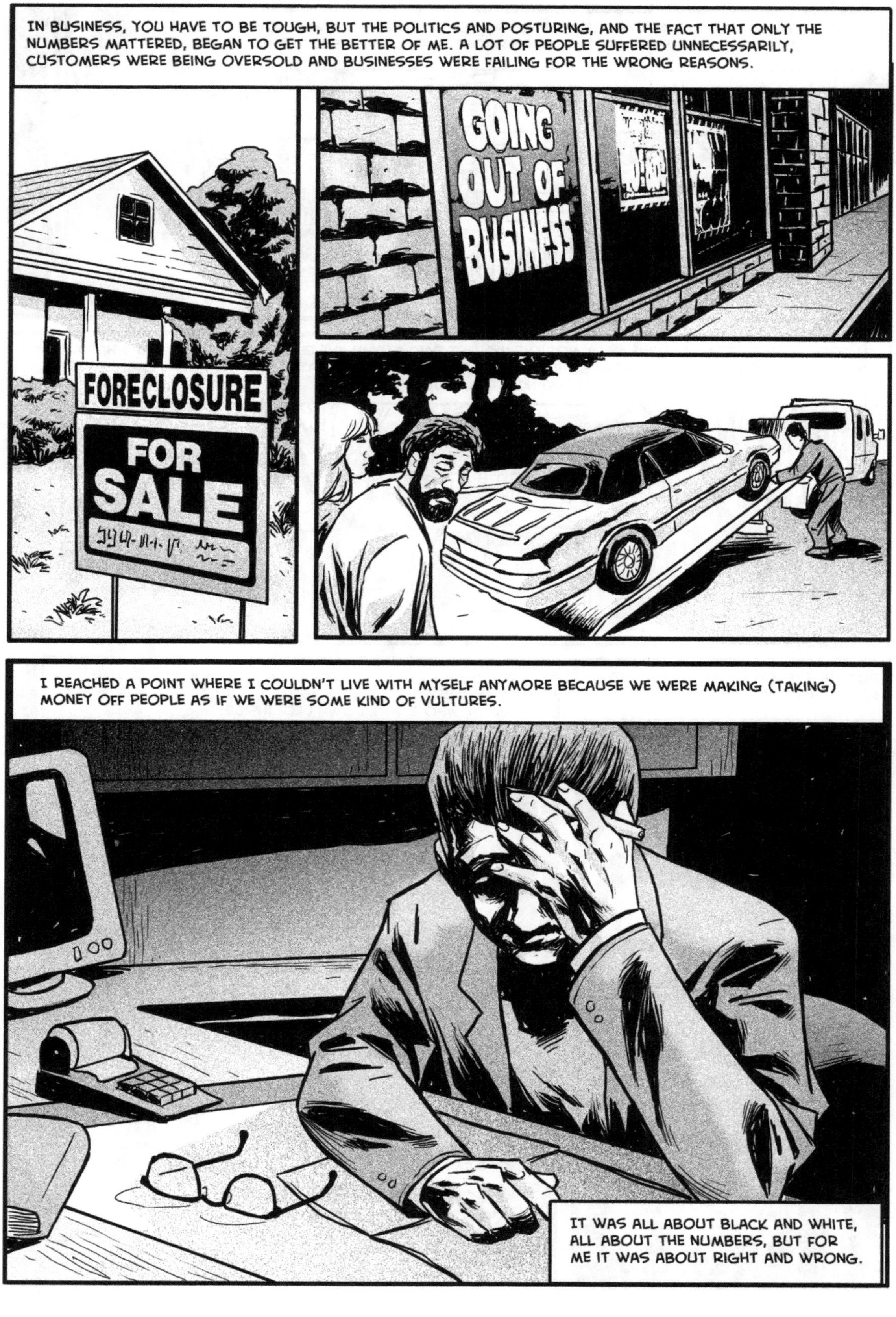
IN BUSINESS, YOU HAVE TO BE TOUGH, BUT THE POLITICS AND POSTURING, AND THE FACT THAT ONLY THE NUMBERS MATTERED, BEGAN TO GET THE BETTER OF ME. A LOT OF PEOPLE SUFFERED UNNECESSARILY, CUSTOMERS WERE BEING OVERSOLD AND BUSINESSES WERE FAILING FOR THE WRONG REASONS.
FORECLOSURE
FOR SALE
GOING OUT OF BUSINESS
I REACHED A POINT WHERE I COULDN'T LIVE WITH MYSELF ANYMORE BECAUSE WE WERE MAKING (TAKING) MONEY OFF PEOPLE AS IF WE WERE SOME KIND OF VULTURES.
IT WAS ALL ABOUT BLACK AND WHITE, ALL ABOUT THE NUMBERS, BUT FOR ME IT WAS ABOUT RIGHT AND WRONG.

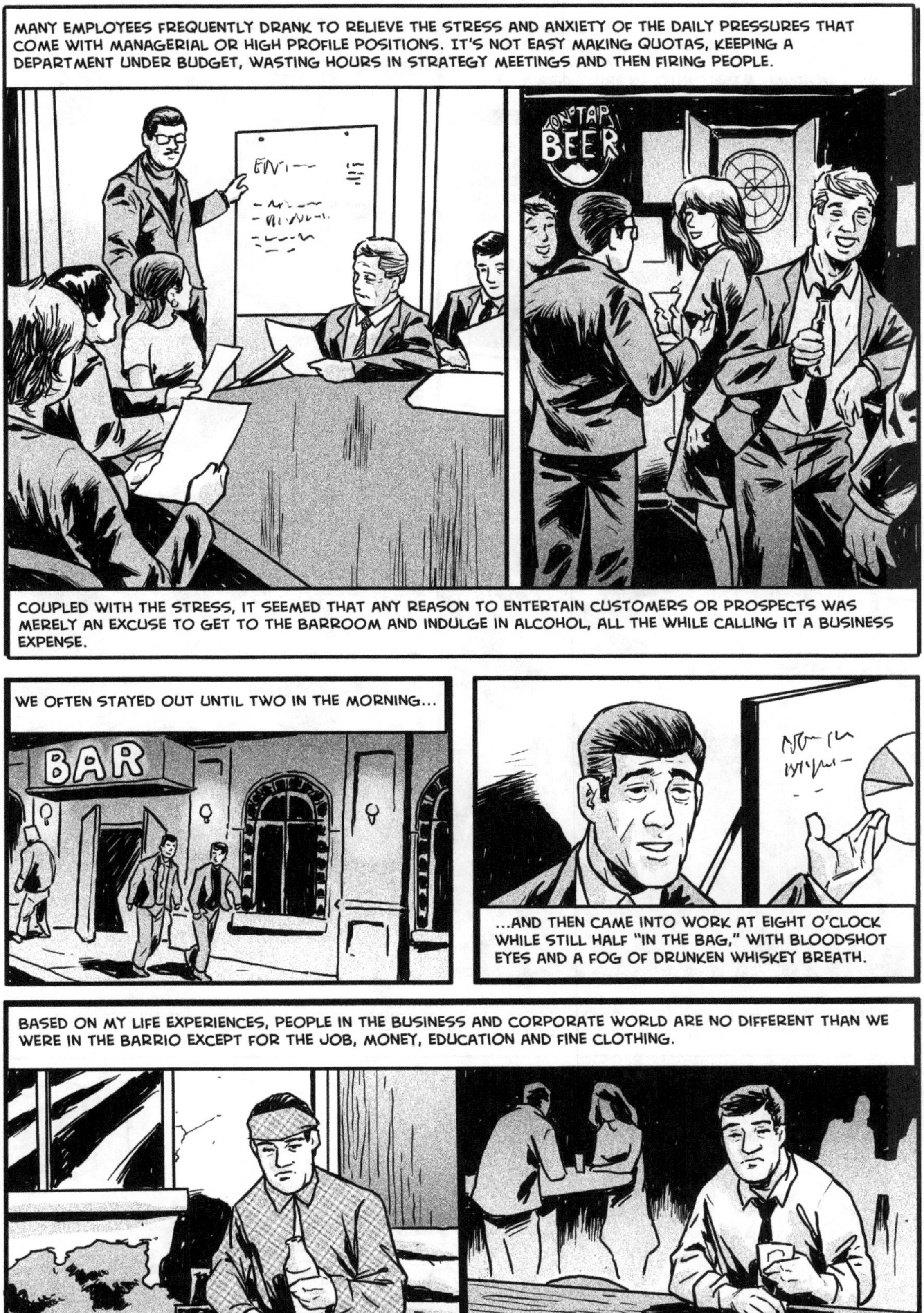
MANY EMPLOYEES FREQUENTLY DRANK TO RELIEVE THE STRESS AND ANXIETY OF THE DAILY PRESSURES THAT COME WITH MANAGERIAL OR HIGH PROFILE POSITIONS. IT'S NOT EASY MAKING QUOTAS, KEEPING A DEPARTMENT UNDER BUDGET, WASTING HOURS IN STRATEGY MEETINGS AND THEN FIRING PEOPLE.
ON TAP
BEER
COUPLED WITH THE STRESS, IT SEEMED THAT ANY REASON TO ENTERTAIN CUSTOMERS OR PROSPECTS WAS MERELY AN EXCUSE TO GET TO THE BARROOM AND INDULGE IN ALCOHOL, ALL THE WHILE CALLING IT A BUSINESS EXPENSE.
WE OFTEN STAYED OUT UNTIL TWO IN THE MORNING...
BAR
...AND THEN CAME INTO WORK AT EIGHT O'CLOCK WHILE STILL HALF "IN THE BAG," WITH BLOODSHOT EYES AND A FOG OF DRUNKEN WHISKEY BREATH.
BASED ON MY LIFE EXPERIENCES, PEOPLE IN THE BUSINESS AND CORPORATE WORLD ARE NO DIFFERENT THAN WE WERE IN THE BARRIO EXCEPT FOR THE JOB, MONEY, EDUCATION AND FINE CLOTHING.

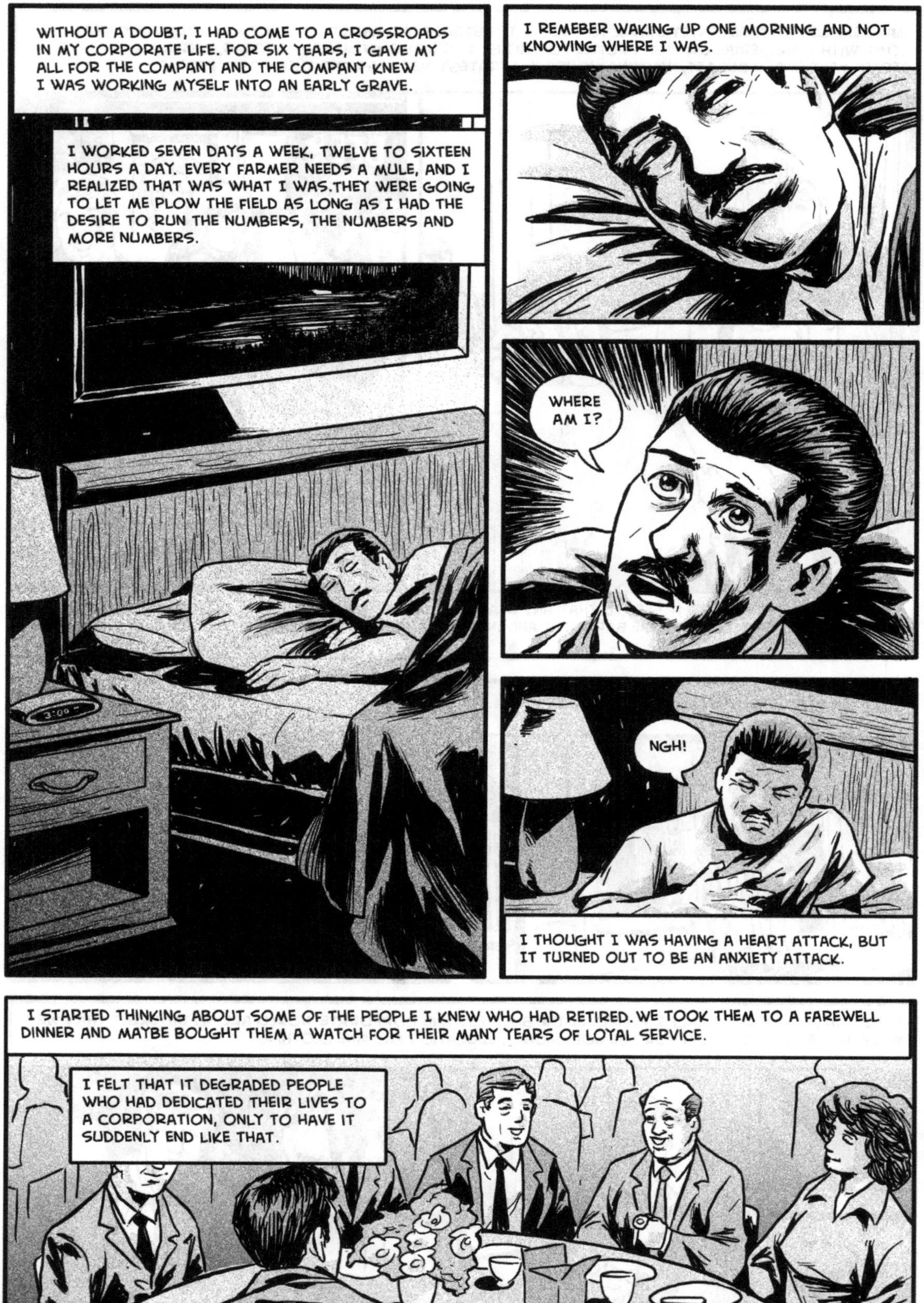
WITHOUT A DOUBT, I HAD COME TO A CROSSROADS IN MY CORPORATE LIFE. FOR SIX YEARS, I GAVE MY ALL FOR THE COMPANY AND THE COMPANY KNEW I WAS WORKING MYSELF INTO AN EARLY GRAVE.
I WORKED SEVEN DAYS A WEEK, TWELVE TO SIXTEEN HOURS A DAY. EVERY FARMER NEEDS A MULE, AND I REALIZED THAT WAS WHAT I WAS.THEY WERE GOING TO LET ME PLOW THE FIELD AS LONG AS I HAD THE DESIRE TO RUN THE NUMBERS, THE NUMBERS AND MORE NUMBERS.
I REMEBER WAKING UP ONE MORNING AND NOT KNOWING WHERE I WAS.
WHERE AM I?
NGH!
I THOUGHT I WAS HAVING A HEART ATTACK, BUT IT TURNED OUT TO BE AN ANXIETY ATTACK.
I STARTED THINKING ABOUT SOME OF THE PEOPLE I KNEW WHO HAD RETIRED. WE TOOK THEM TO A FAREWELL DINNER AND MAYBE BOUGHT THEM A WATCH FOR THEIR MANY YEARS OF LOYAL SERVICE.
I FELT THAT IT DEGRADED PEOPLE WHO HAD DEDICATED THEIR LIVES TO A CORPORATION, ONLY TO HAVE IT SUDDENLY END LIKE THAT.

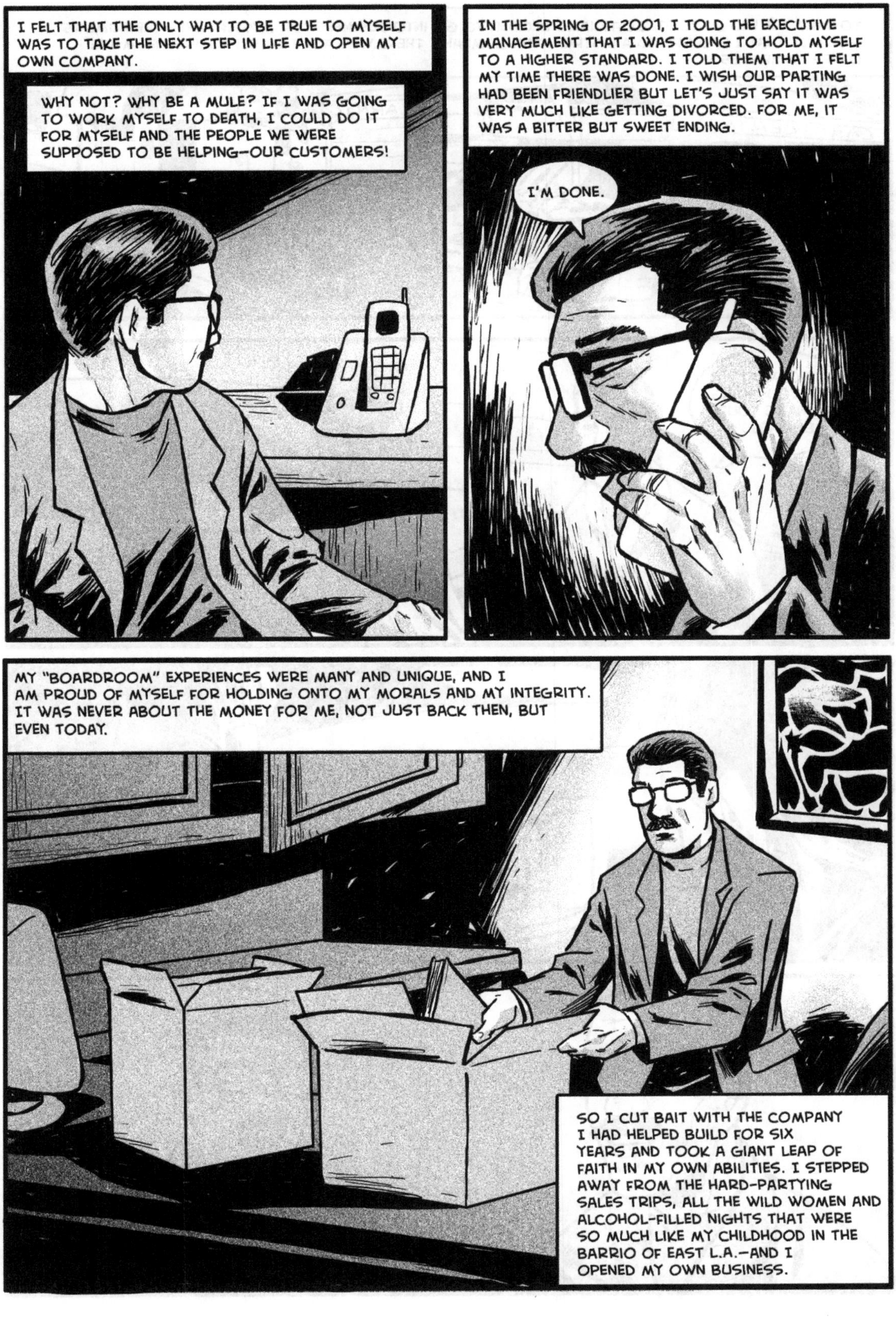
I FELT THAT THE ONLY WAY TO BE TRUE TO MYSELF WAS TO TAKE THE NEXT STEP IN LIFE AND OPEN MY OWN COMPANY.
WHY NOT? WHY BE A MULE? IF I WAS GOING TO WORK MYSELF TO DEATH, I COULD DO IT FOR MYSELF AND THE PEOPLE WE WERE SUPPOSED TO BE HELPING—OUR CUSTOMERS!
IN THE SPRING OF 2001, I TOLD THE EXECUTIVE MANAGEMENT THAT I WAS GOING TO HOLD MYSELF TO A HIGHER STANDARD. I TOLD THEM THAT I FELT MY TIME THERE WAS DONE. I WISH OUR PARTING HAD BEEN FRIENDLIER BUT LET'S JUST SAY IT WAS VERY MUCH LIKE GETTING DIVORCED. FOR ME, IT WAS A BITTER BUT SWEET ENDING.
I'M DONE.
MY "BOARDROOM" EXPERIENCES WERE MANY AND UNIQUE, AND I AM PROUD OF MYSELF FOR HOLDING ONTO MY MORALS AND MY INTEGRITY. IT WAS NEVER ABOUT THE MONEY FOR ME, NOT JUST BACK THEN, BUT EVEN TODAY.
SO I CUT BAIT WITH THE COMPANY I HAD HELPED BUILD FOR SIX YEARS AND TOOK A GIANT LEAP OF FAITH IN MY OWN ABILITIES. I STEPPED AWAY FROM THE HARD-PARTYING SALES TRIPS, ALL THE WILD WOMEN AND ALCOHOL-FILLED NIGHTS THAT WERE SO MUCH LIKE MY CHILDHOOD IN THE BARRIO OF EAST L.A.—AND I OPENED MY OWN BUSINESS.

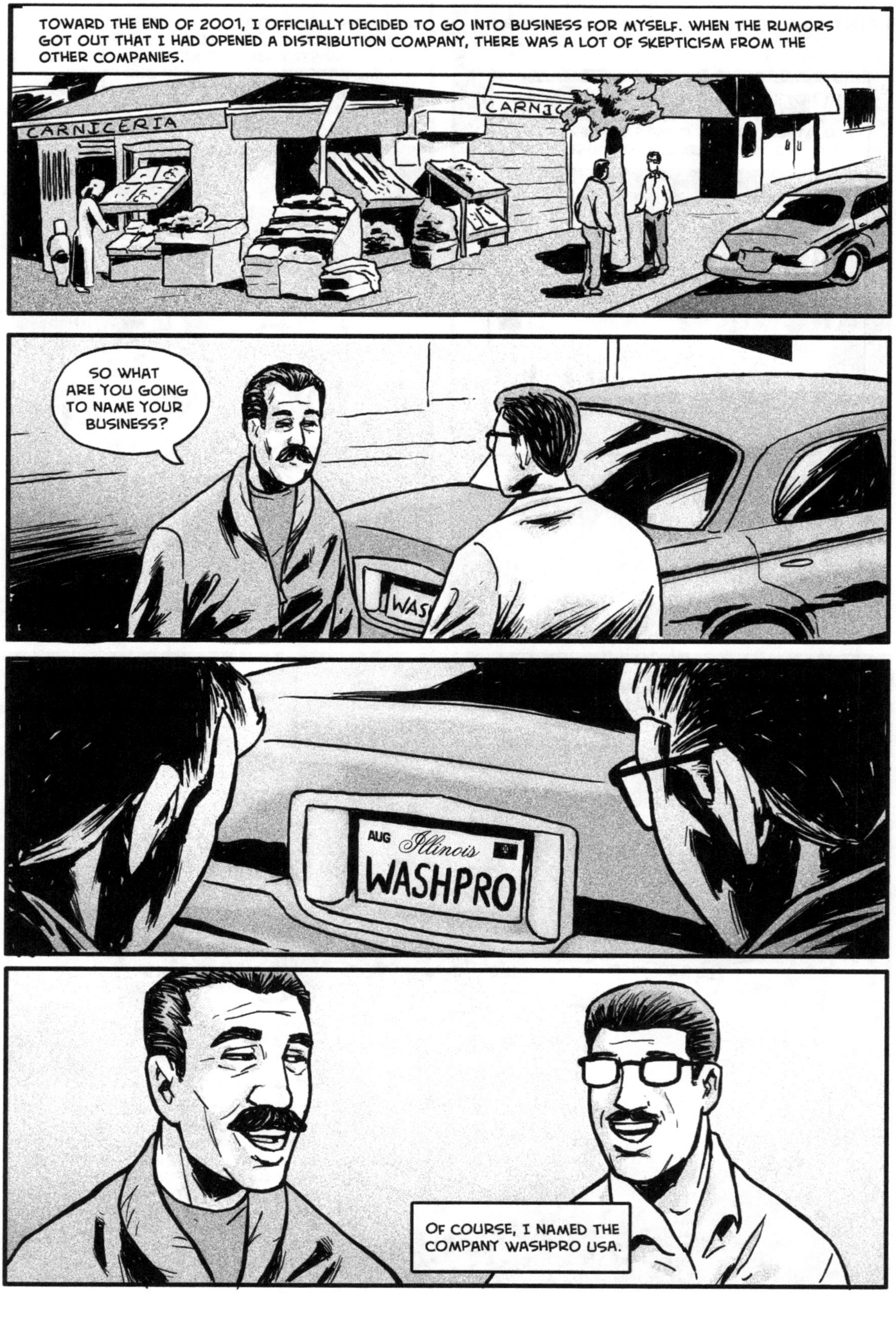
TOWARD THE END OF 2001, I OFFICIALLY DECIDED TO GO INTO BUSINESS FOR MYSELF. WHEN THE RUMORS GOT OUT THAT I HAD OPENED A DISTRIBUTION COMPANY, THERE WAS A LOT OF SKEPTICISM FROM THE OTHER COMPANIES.
CARNICERIA
SO WHAT ARE YOU GOING TO NAME YOUR BUSINESS?
AUG Illinois
WASHPRO
OF COURSE, I NAMED THE COMPANY WASHPRO USA.

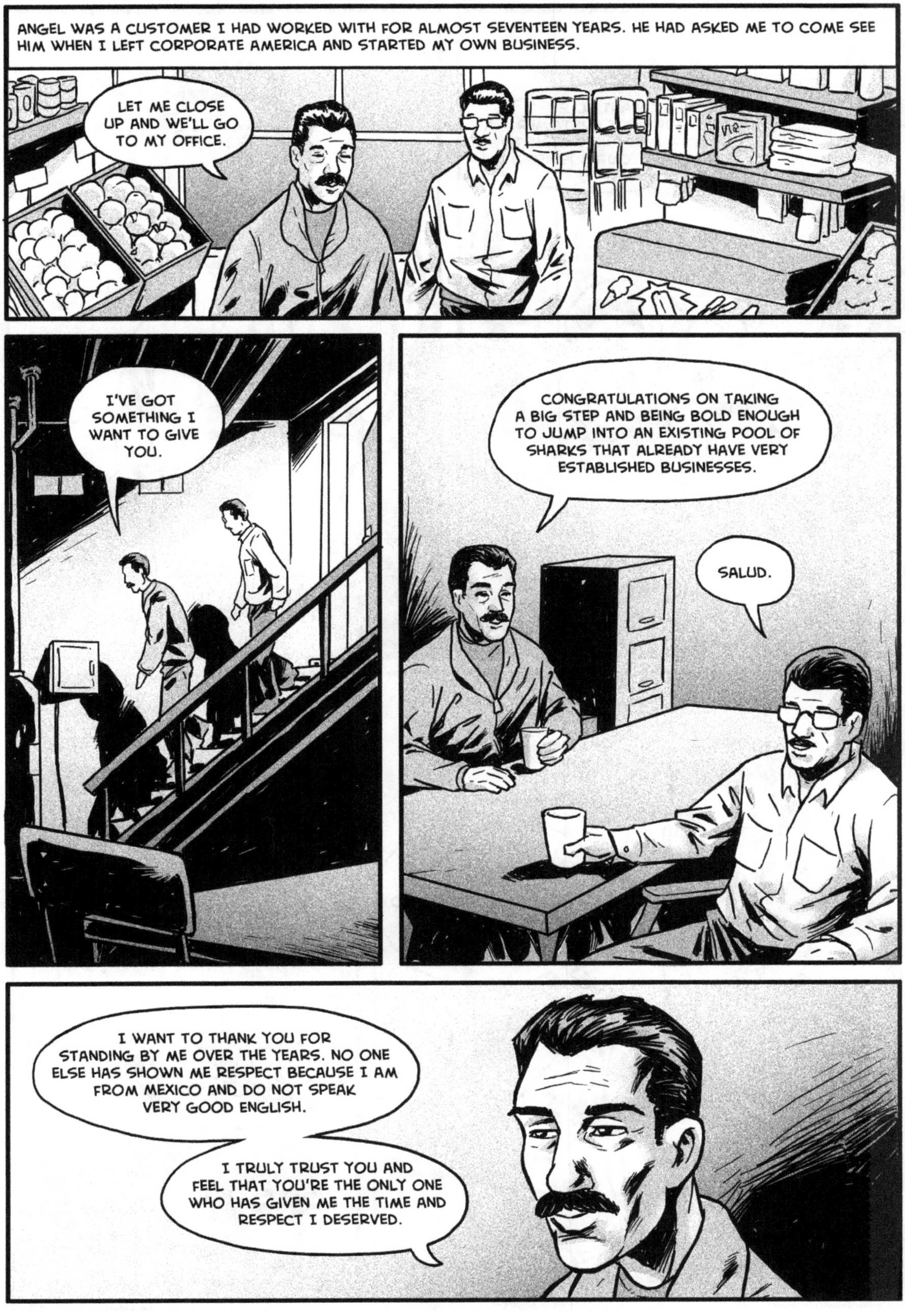
ANGEL WAS A CUSTOMER I HAD WORKED WITH FOR ALMOST SEVENTEEN YEARS. HE HAD ASKED ME TO COME SEE HIM WHEN I LEFT CORPORATE AMERICA AND STARTED MY OWN BUSINESS.
LET ME CLOSE UP AND WE'LL GO TO MY OFFICE.
I'VE GOT SOMETHING I WANT TO GIVE YOU.
CONGRATULATIONS ON TAKING A BIG STEP AND BEING BOLD ENOUGH TO JUMP INTO AN EXISTING POOL OF SHARKS THAT ALREADY HAVE VERY ESTABLISHED BUSINESSES.
SALUD.
I WANT TO THANK YOU FOR STANDING BY ME OVER THE YEARS. NO ONE ELSE HAS SHOWN ME RESPECT BECAUSE I AM FROM MEXICO AND DO NOT SPEAK VERY GOOD ENGLISH.
I TRULY TRUST YOU AND FEEL THAT YOU'RE THE ONLY ONE WHO HAS GIVEN ME THE TIME AND RESPECT I DESERVED.

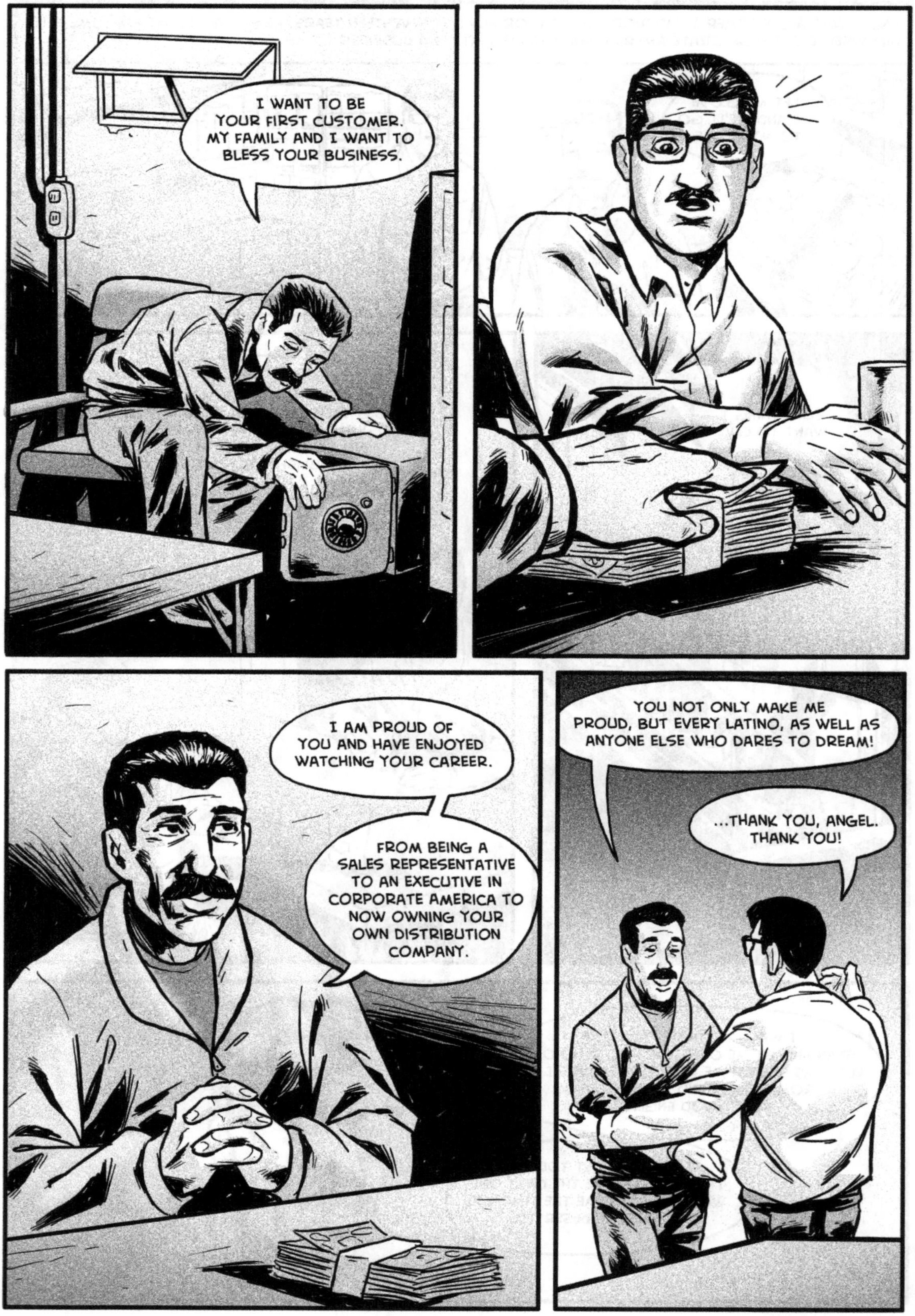
I WANT TO BE YOUR FIRST CUSTOMER. MY FAMILY AND I WANT TO BLESS YOUR BUSINESS.
I AM PROUD OF YOU AND HAVE ENJOYED WATCHING YOUR CAREER.
FROM BEING A SALES REPRESENTATIVE TO AN EXECUTIVE IN CORPORATE AMERICA TO NOW OWNING YOUR OWN DISTRIBUTION COMPANY.
YOU NOT ONLY MAKE ME PROUD, BUT EVERY LATINO, AS WELL AS ANYONE ELSE WHO DARES TO DREAM!
...THANK YOU, ANGEL. THANK YOU!

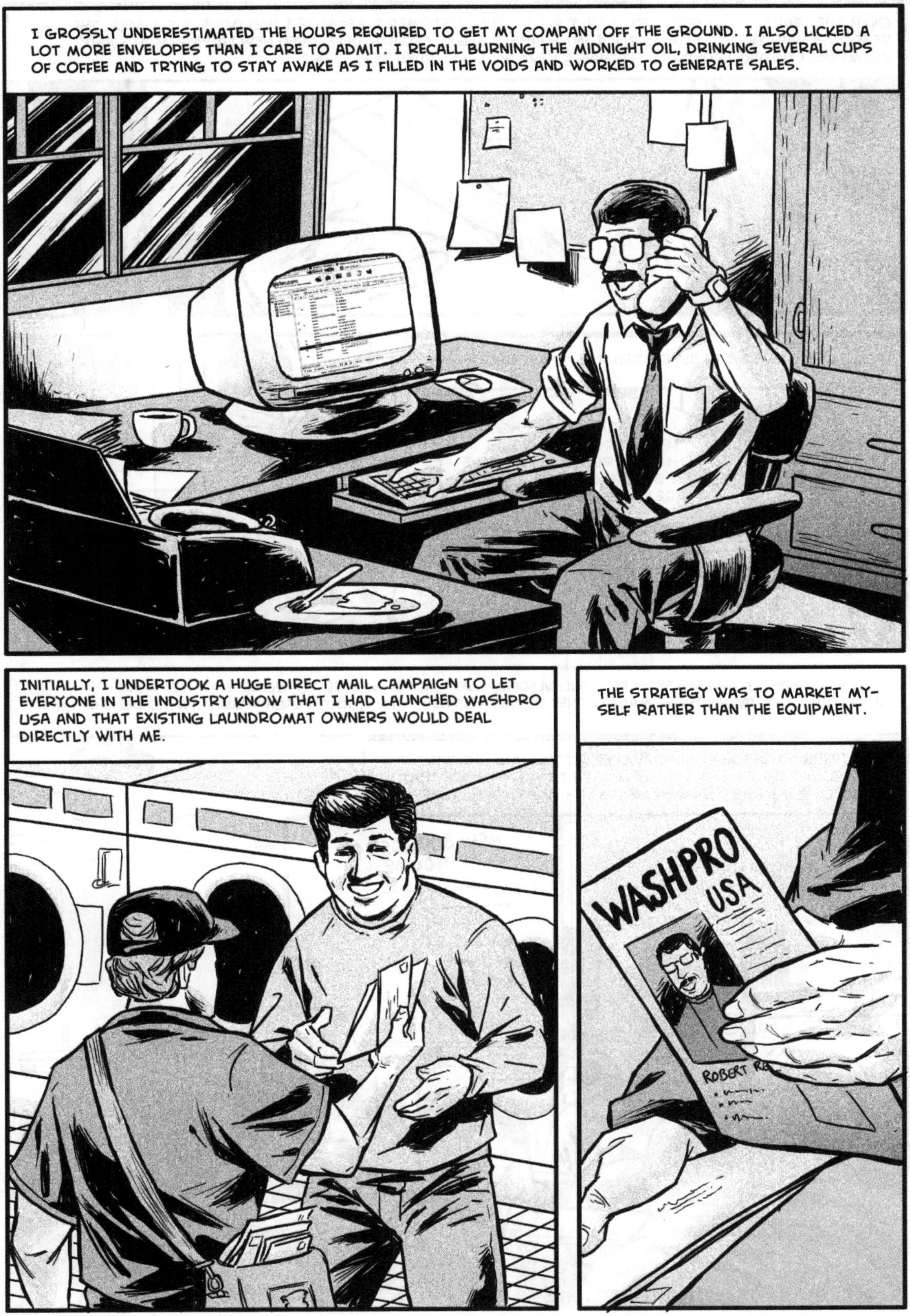
I GROSSLY UNDERESTIMATED THE HOURS REQUIRED TO GET MY COMPANY OFF THE GROUND. I ALSO LICKED A LOT MORE ENVELOPES THAN I CARE TO ADMIT. I RECALL BURNING THE MIDNIGHT OIL, DRINKING SEVERAL CUPS OF COFFEE AND TRYING TO STAY AWAKE AS I FILLED IN THE VOIDS AND WORKED TO GENERATE SALES.
INITIALLY, I UNDERTOOK A HUGE DIRECT MAIL CAMPAIGN TO LET EVERYONE IN THE INDUSTRY KNOW THAT I HAD LAUNCHED WASHPRO USA AND THAT EXISTING LAUNDROMAT OWNERS WOULD DEAL DIRECTLY WITH ME.
THE STRATEGY WAS TO MARKET MYSELF RATHER THAN THE EQUIPMENT.
WASHPRO
USA
ROBERT

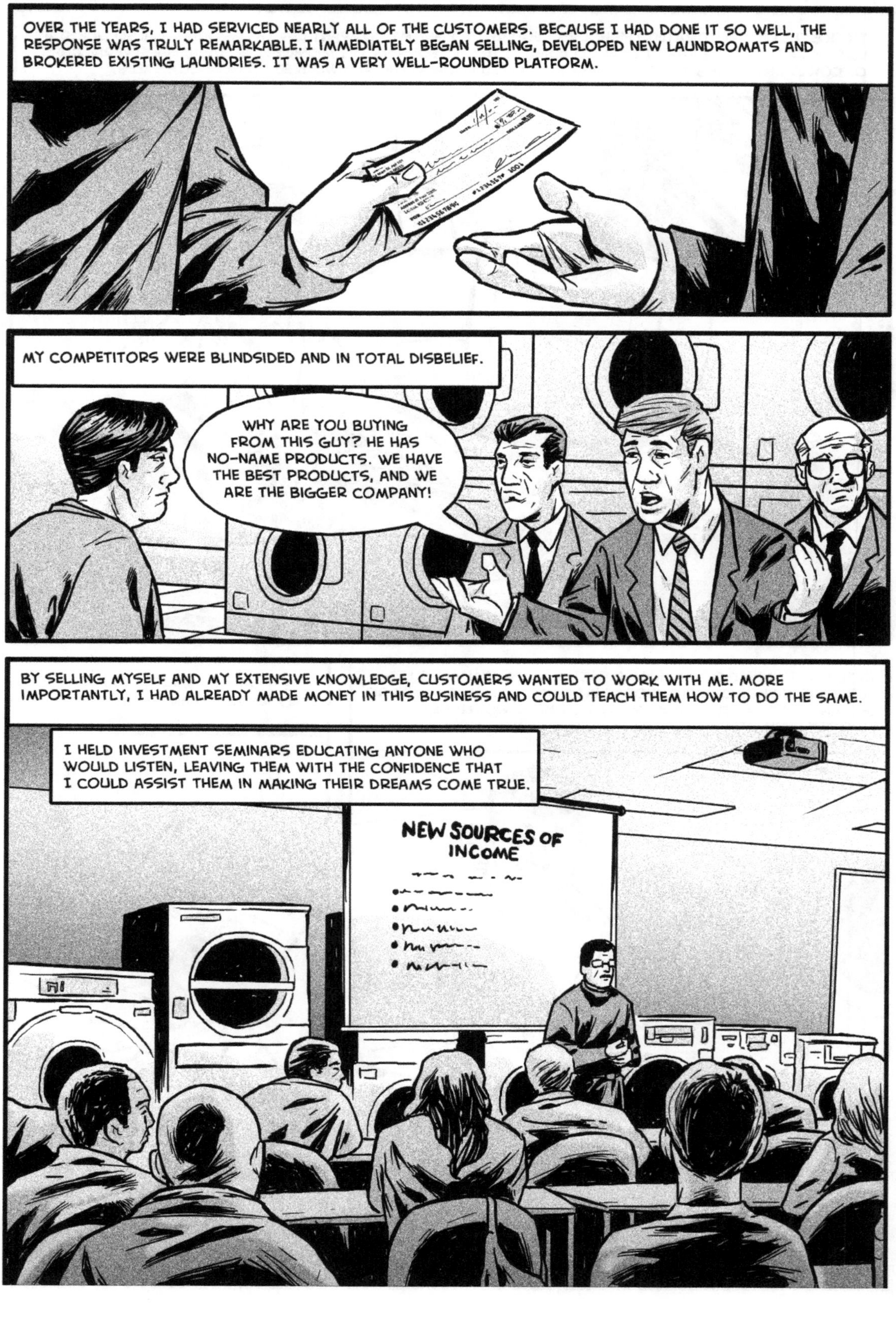
OVER THE YEARS, I HAD SERVICED NEARLY ALL OF THE CUSTOMERS. BECAUSE I HAD DONE IT SO WELL, THE RESPONSE WAS TRULY REMARKABLE. I IMMEDIATELY BEGAN SELLING, DEVELOPED NEW LAUNDROMATS AND BROKERED EXISTING LAUNDRIES. IT WAS A VERY WELL-ROUNDED PLATFORM.
MY COMPETITORS WERE BLINDSIDED AND IN TOTAL DISBELIEF.
WHY ARE YOU BUYING FROM THIS GUY? HE HAS NO-NAME PRODUCTS. WE HAVE THE BEST PRODUCTS, AND WE ARE THE BIGGER COMPANY!
BY SELLING MYSELF AND MY EXTENSIVE KNOWLEDGE, CUSTOMERS WANTED TO WORK WITH ME. MORE IMPORTANTLY, I HAD ALREADY MADE MONEY IN THIS BUSINESS AND COULD TEACH THEM HOW TO DO THE SAME.
I HELD INVESTMENT SEMINARS EDUCATING ANYONE WHO WOULD LISTEN, LEAVING THEM WITH THE CONFIDENCE THAT I COULD ASSIST THEM IN MAKING THEIR DREAMS COME TRUE.
NEW SOURCES OF INCOME

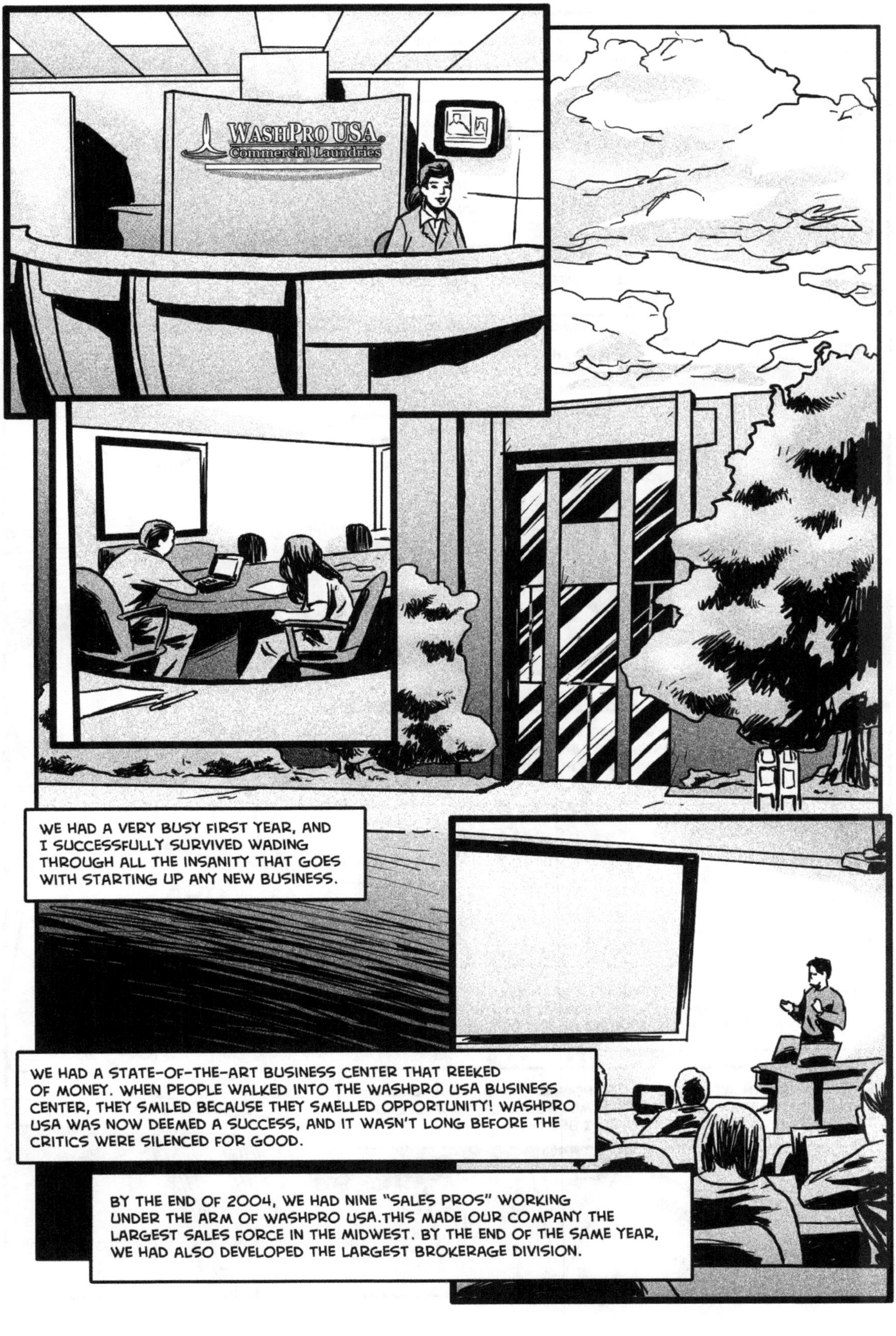
WASHPRO USA
Commercial Laundries
WE HAD A VERY BUSY FIRST YEAR, AND I SUCCESSFULLY SURVIVED WADING THROUGH ALL THE INSANITY THAT GOES WITH STARTING UP ANY NEW BUSINESS.
WE HAD A STATE-OF-THE-ART BUSINESS CENTER THAT REEKED OF MONEY. WHEN PEOPLE WALKED INTO THE WASHPRO USA BUSINESS CENTER, THEY SMILED BECAUSE THEY SMELLED OPPORTUNITY! WASHPRO USA WAS NOW DEEMED A SUCCESS, AND IT WASN'T LONG BEFORE THE CRITICS WERE SILENCED FOR GOOD.
BY THE END OF 2004, WE HAD NINE "SALES PROS" WORKING UNDER THE ARM OF WASHPRO USA.THIS MADE OUR COMPANY THE LARGEST SALES FORCE IN THE MIDWEST. BY THE END OF THE SAME YEAR, WE HAD ALSO DEVELOPED THE LARGEST BROKERAGE DIVISION.

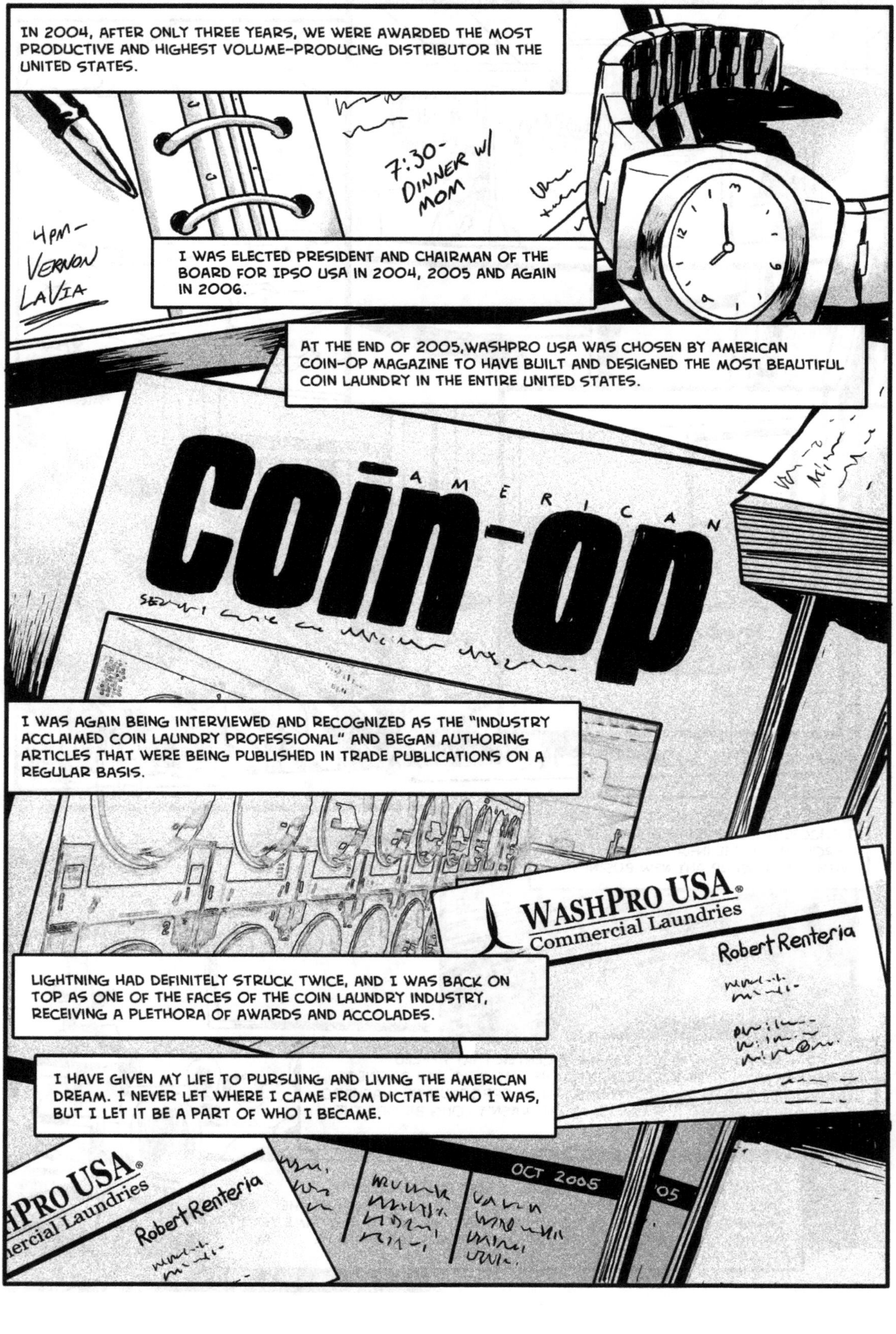
IN 2004, AFTER ONLY THREE YEARS, WE WERE AWARDED THE MOST PRODUCTIVE AND HIGHEST VOLUME-PRODUCING DISTRIBUTOR IN THE UNITED STATES.
7:30- DINNER W/ MOM
4pm- VERNON LAVIA
I WAS ELECTED PRESIDENT AND CHAIRMAN OF THE BOARD FOR IPSO USA IN 2004, 2005 AND AGAIN IN 2006.
AT THE END OF 2005,WASHPRO USA WAS CHOSEN BY AMERICAN COIN-OP MAGAZINE TO HAVE BUILT AND DESIGNED THE MOST BEAUTIFUL COIN LAUNDRY IN THE ENTIRE UNITED STATES.
AMERICAN Coin-op
I WAS AGAIN BEING INTERVIEWED AND RECOGNIZED AS THE "INDUSTRY ACCLAIMED COIN LAUNDRY PROFESSIONAL" AND BEGAN AUTHORING ARTICLES THAT WERE BEING PUBLISHED IN TRADE PUBLICATIONS ON A REGULAR BASIS.
WASHPRO USA®
Commercial Laundries
Robert Renteria
LIGHTNING HAD DEFINITELY STRUCK TWICE, AND I WAS BACK ON TOP AS ONE OF THE FACES OF THE COIN LAUNDRY INDUSTRY, RECEIVING A PLETHORA OF AWARDS AND ACCOLADES.
I HAVE GIVEN MY LIFE TO PURSUING AND LIVING THE AMERICAN DREAM. I NEVER LET WHERE I CAME FROM DICTATE WHO I WAS, BUT I LET IT BE A PART OF WHO I BECAME.
OCT 2005
HPRO USA®
ercial Laundries
Robert Renteria

EPILOGUE

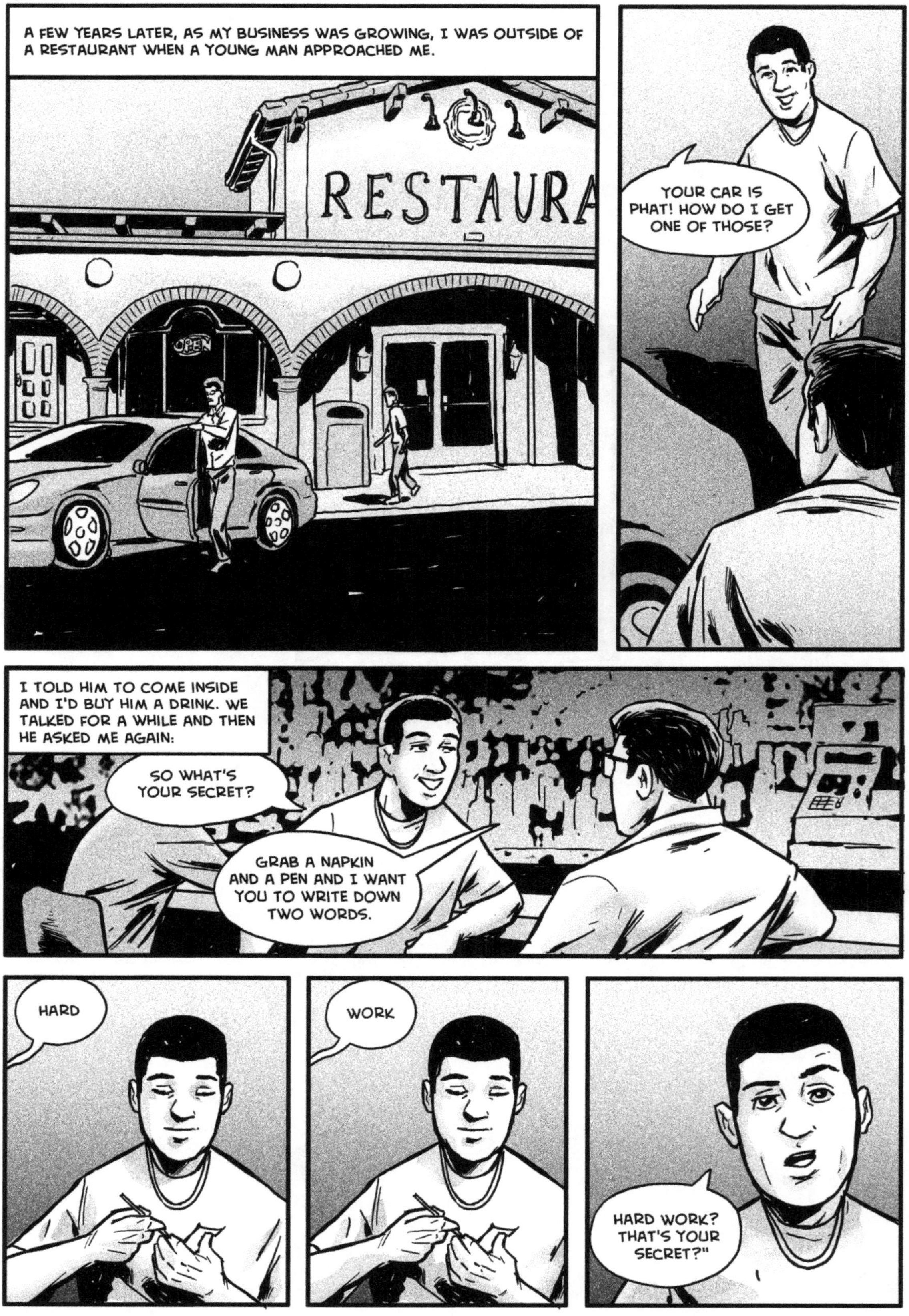
A FEW YEARS LATER, AS MY BUSINESS WAS GROWING, I WAS OUTSIDE OF A RESTAURANT WHEN A YOUNG MAN APPROACHED ME.
RESTAURA
OPEN
YOUR CAR IS PHAT! HOW DO I GET ONE OF THOSE?
I TOLD HIM TO COME INSIDE AND I'D BUY HIM A DRINK. WE TALKED FOR A WHILE AND THEN HE ASKED ME AGAIN:
SO WHAT'S YOUR SECRET?
GRAB A NAPKIN AND A PEN AND I WANT YOU TO WRITE DOWN TWO WORDS.
HARD
WORK
HARD WORK? THAT'S YOUR SECRET?"

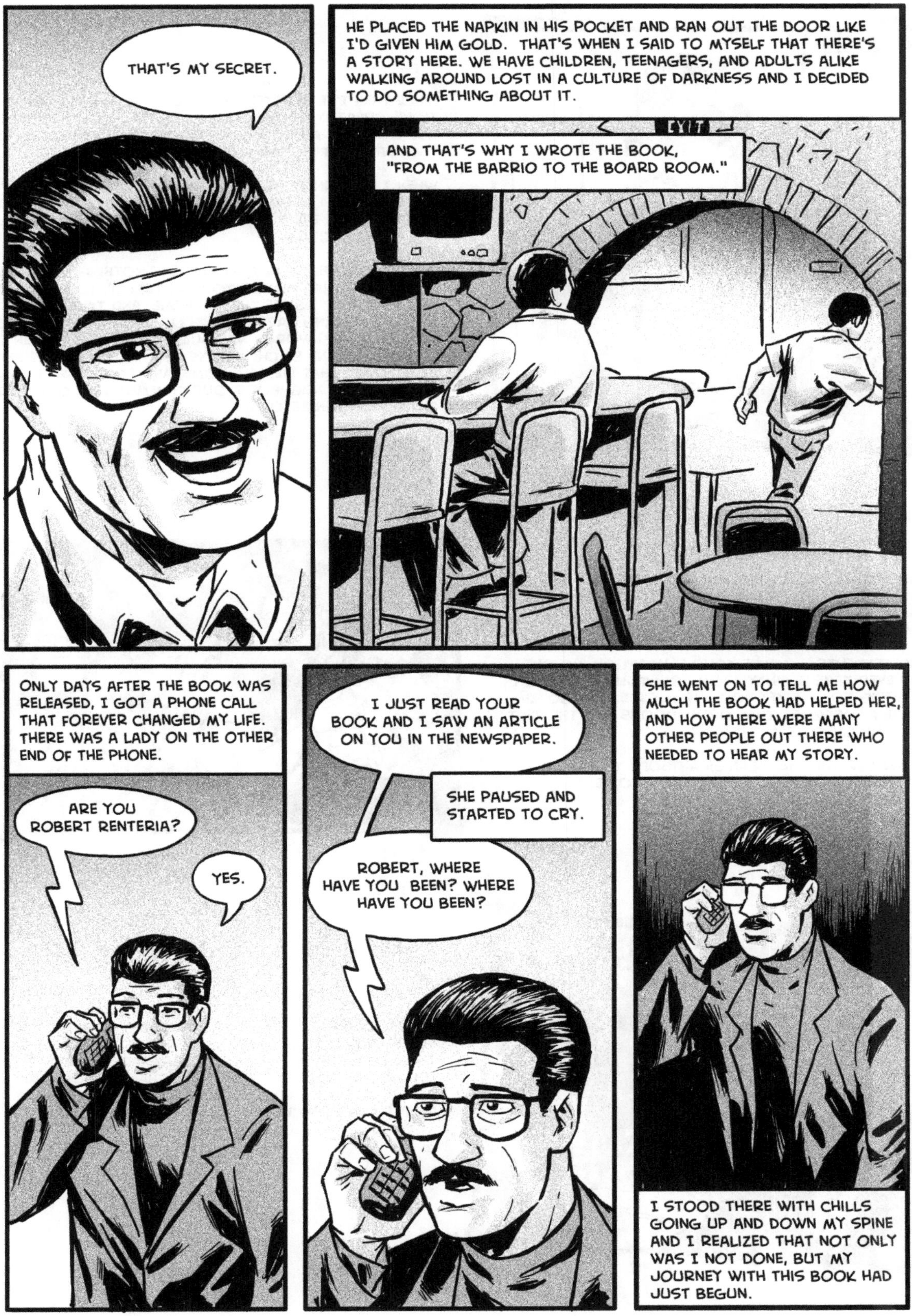
THAT'S MY SECRET.
HE PLACED THE NAPKIN IN HIS POCKET AND RAN OUT THE DOOR LIKE I'D GIVEN HIM GOLD. THAT'S WHEN I SAID TO MYSELF THAT THERE'S A STORY HERE. WE HAVE CHILDREN, TEENAGERS, AND ADULTS ALIKE WALKING AROUND LOST IN A CULTURE OF DARKNESS AND I DECIDED TO DO SOMETHING ABOUT IT.
AND THAT'S WHY I WROTE THE BOOK, "FROM THE BARRIO TO THE BOARD ROOM."
ONLY DAYS AFTER THE BOOK WAS RELEASED, I GOT A PHONE CALL THAT FOREVER CHANGED MY LIFE. THERE WAS A LADY ON THE OTHER END OF THE PHONE.
ARE YOU ROBERT RENTERIA?
YES.
I JUST READ YOUR BOOK AND I SAW AN ARTICLE ON YOU IN THE NEWSPAPER.
SHE PAUSED AND STARTED TO CRY.
ROBERT, WHERE HAVE YOU BEEN? WHERE HAVE YOU BEEN?
SHE WENT ON TO TELL ME HOW MUCH THE BOOK HAD HELPED HER, AND HOW THERE WERE MANY OTHER PEOPLE OUT THERE WHO NEEDED TO HEAR MY STORY.
I STOOD THERE WITH CHILLS GOING UP AND DOWN MY SPINE AND I REALIZED THAT NOT ONLY WAS I NOT DONE, BUT MY JOURNEY WITH THIS BOOK HAD JUST BEGUN.

SINCE THEN I'VE STARTED THE "FROM THE BARRIO FOUNDA-TION", CREATED A CURRICULUM FOR TEACHERS TO HELP THEM USE THE BOOK AS A TEACHING TOOL, AND I'VE SPOKEN TO THOUSANDS OF PEOPLE ALL AROUND THE COUNTRY.

WHEN I LOOK INTO THE EYES OF THOSE I'M WORKING WITH I SEE HOPE AND I SEE DREAMS. I SEE POSSIBILITIES WAITING TO HAPPEN AND IN THE STUDENTS I MEET I SEE THE FUTURE LEAD-ERS OF TOMORROW.

I'M HERE TO TELL YOU THAT THERE IS NOTHING MORE IMPOR-TANT IN LIFE THAN FAMILY. YOU PROTECT IT, YOU RESPECT IT, AND YOU DON'T ABUSE THE PRIVILEGE. AND TAKE CARE OF ONE ANOTHER. TAKING CARE OF EACH OTHER WAS HOW THE FOUN-DATION OF THIS WORLD WAS BUILT. SO LET'S BUILD ON THAT FOUNDATION AND BE CHAMPIONS OF THIS PLACE. THIS PLACE HERE TODAY THAT WE CALL HOME, AND TAKE CARE OF OUR FAMILIES, OUR NEIGHBORS, OUR COMMUNITIES, OUR GREAT CITIES AND THEN BEYOND!

HARD WORK, DEDICATION, AND EDUCATION ARE THE THREE SECRETS TO SUCCESS. DON'T LET WHERE YOU CAME FROM DICTATE WHO YOU ARE, BUT LET IT BE PART OF WHO YOU BECOME. RESPECT YOUR ROOTS.

AND STUDENTS -- VALUE YOUR EDUCTATION. NO ONE CAN EVER TAKE IT AWAY FROM YOU. YOUR EDUCATION IS GOING TO BE A KEY TO YOUR FUTURE. IT'S GOING TO BE A PASSPORT THAT OPENS DOORS FOR THE REST OF YOUR LIVES.

REMEMBER THIS: YOU CAN BE ANYBODY YOU WANT TO BE! YOU CAN BE ANYBODY YOU WANT TO BE!

I'M ALSO HERE TO TELL YOU THAT GANG-BANGING AND VIOLENCE IS NOT A LIFESTYLE, BUT A DEATH-STYLE. I'M TIRED OF WATCHING PEOPLE PUT BANDAIDS ON BUL-LET WOUNDS. IT'S MY GOAL TO EXCHANGE THE BARRIO BOOKS FOR ALL THE GUNS, KNIVES, DRUGS, NEEDLES, BOOZE AND EVEN CIGARETTES.

USE MY STORY AS A ROAD MAP TO AVOID THE DETOURS THAT I TOOK IN MY LIFE. HELP ME TO SHARE THIS MESSAGE, OUR MESSAGE, WITH YOUR FAMILY, YOUR TEACHERS AND YOUR FRIENDS. AND THEN TELL EACH OTHER YOUR OWN STORIES. WE ALL COME FROM SOMEWHERE AND WE'RE ALL GOING SOMEPLACE.

BE PROUD OF WHO YOU ARE AND DON'T LET ANYBODY EVER TELL YOU THAT YOU CAN'T DO SOMETHING. BECAUSE AS LONG AS YOU HAVE A CORAZON, A HEART, YOU ALWAYS HAVE A CHANCE. YOU ALWAYS HAVE A CHANCE.

THANK YOU. MAY GOD BLESS YOU. GRACIAS! QUE DIOS TE BENDIGA! I LOVE YOU AND THERE'S NOTHING YOU CAN DO ABOUT IT!

ROBERT J. RENTERIA
CHAIRMAN
FROM THE BARRIO FOUNDATION

ROBERT J. RENTERIA

is a successful businessman turned author of *From the Barrio to the Board Room*, who is using his memoir and comic book with youth across America to replace violence, delinquency, gangs and drugs with education, pride, accomplishment, and self esteem. He dedicated his life to sharing his story with thousands of others so that they, too, can help break the vicious cycle of poverty through hard work, determination and education. His book, comic book and the accompanying curriculum, are forming our "leaders of tomorrow" by helping them to find their identity, establish core values, set goals for themselves, prioritize education, and strive to reach their full potential.

Renteria has been the keynote speaker at the Hispanic Heritage Reception for Illinois Secretary of State Jesse White, where he was recognized for his achievements as a Latino author. He has also presented at the Illinois Association of School Social Workers, the Chicago Principals and Administrators Association annual conference, McDonald's Hamburger University, the Hispanic National Bar Association in Chicago, the Illinois Legislative Latino Caucus Foundation, and the Chicago Public Schools. In July 2010 Robert was announced as a finalist for Chicago Latino Professional of the Year. Robert has been profiled in major media, including *WGN Midday News, Univision, La Raza, Hispanic Executive Quarterly, Hoy, WGN Adelante Chicago,* more than two dozen radio stations, including Chicago Public Radio and numerous newspapers and magazines. Robert is supported by political figures (at the local, state and national level), business owners, corporations, University Professors, and middle and high school teachers and principals who share his universal message that everyone has the right to live the American Dream through education, determination, and hard-work!

COREY MICHAEL BLAKE

has starred in campaigns and written and published books that have been profiled in the New York Times, Los Angeles Times, Sports Illustrated, Variety and on NBC, WGN and Good Morning America among hundreds of other print, radio, and television outlets. His work has won Addy, Belding, Bronze Lion and London International Advertising awards and he has been published in Writer Magazine, Script Magazine and on StartUp Nation. Corey began his career as the face of commercial campaigns for more than a dozen Fortune 500 and Fortune 100 companies, before venturing off to filmmaking and eventually writing. He is the co-author of numerous books, including *Edge! A Leadership Story* (Finalist 2008 National Best Books Awards) and *From the Barrio to the Board Room*, which is being used throughout the Chicago Public School District and in schools and youth prisons around the country to inspire at-risk youth. He founded Round Table Companies and Writers of the Round Table Press to focus on his love of building creative brands. Corey holds a BFA from Millikin University.

SHANE CLESTER

At six years old, Shane Clester realized that most people aren't happy with their jobs. Even as he drew robots just to see if he could, he decided that he would turn his artistic play into work. As Shane grew older and studied the nuances of art, his initial excitement evolved into fascination. He was compelled by the replication of life through seemingly limited tools, and embarked on a quest to learn technical proficiency. In the early 2000s, Shane studied briefly under Jim Garrison, well-known for his art anatomy and technical skills. Shane then relocated from Arizona to California, where he learned a powerful lesson: You have to study to be an artist, and then you have to learn the business of being an artist. Over the course of the next several years, he broadened his portfolio to include youth-oriented art and comic books, and sourced clients by attending conferences and book fairs. Some of his clients have included leading comic book publisher IDW, Hasbro, Scholastic, Macmillan, and Times of London. Of his many projects, Shane is particularly proud of *Skate Farm: Volume 2*, a graphic novel he produced, and *Mi Barrio*. Look for Shane's next release, a comic book version of Larry Winget's best-selling *Shut Up, Stop Whining & Get a Life* (Writers of the Round Table Press, 2011).

Look for these other titles from SmarterComics and Writers of the Round Table Press:

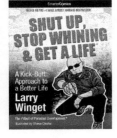

SHUT UP, STOP WHINING & GET A LIFE
A Kick-Butt Approach to a Better Life
Larry Winget

Shut Up, Stop Whining & Get a Life from SmarterComics
(December 2010) by Larry Winget Illustrated by Shane Clester
Internationally renowned success philosopher, business speaker, and humorist, Larry Winget offers advice that flies in the face of conventional self-help. Shut Up, Stop Whining, and Get a Life from SmarterComics forces all responsibility for every aspect of your life right where it belongs - on you.

THE ART OF WAR
HOW TO BE SUCCESSFUL IN ANY COMPETITION
SUN TZU
IN BUSINESS, SPORTS, POLITICS, OR LIFE!

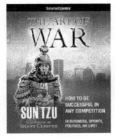

The Art of War from SmarterComics
(September 2010) by Sun Tzu Illustrated by Shane Clester
As true today as when it was written, THE ART OF WAR is a 2,500-year-old classic that is required reading in modern business schools. Penned by the ancient Chinese philosopher and military general Sun Tzu, it reveals how to succeed in any conflict. Read this comic version, and cut to the heart of the message!

THINK & GROW RICH
NAPOLEON HILL

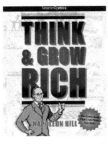

Think and Grow Rich from SmarterComics
(August 2010) by Napoleon Hill Illustrated by Bob Byrne
Think and Grow Rich has sold over 30 million copies and is regarded as the greatest wealth-building guide of all time. Read this comic version and cut to the heart of the message! Written at the advice of millionaire Andrew Carnegie, the book summarizes ideas from over 500 rich and successful people on how to achieve your dreams and get rich doing it. You'll learn money-making secrets - not only what to do but how - laid out in simple steps.

How to Master the Art of Selling from SmarterComics
(February 2011) by Tom Hopkins
With over one million copies sold in it's original version, *How to Master the Art of Selling from SmarterComics* motivates and educates readers to deliver superior sales. After failing during the first six months of his career in sales, Tom Hopkins discovered and applied the very best sales techniques, then earned more than one million dollars in just three years. What turned Tom Hopkins around? The answers are revealed in *How to Master the Art of Selling from SmarterComics*, as Tom explains to readers what the profession of selling is really about and how to succeed beyond their imagination.

For the ebook versions, please visit www.smartercomics.com
For the printed versions, please visit www.roundtablepress.com

THE BOOK THAT INSPIRED THE COMIC

Available at online retailers and at www.fromthebarrio.com

FROM THE BARRIO^{SM}
Foundation

The From the Barrio Foundation is an Illinois not-for-profit corporation that addresses conditions that help youth avoid choices which may lead to violence, delinquency, drug use and gangs. The Foundation promotes education, valuing a sense of pride and accomplishment, and advocates for social values which foster improved self-esteem.

The Foundation, led by Robert Renteria, uses his books -- *From the Barrio to the Board Room* and *Mi Barrio*, and the curriculum, *From the Barrio to the Classroom* -- to help inspire and motivate youth and young adults through education, pride, accomplishment, perseverance, and determination. The books and curriculum enable participants to practice the social values necessary to realize repeated success throughout their lives and to then become effective mentors to others.

For more information visit: www.fromthebarrio.com

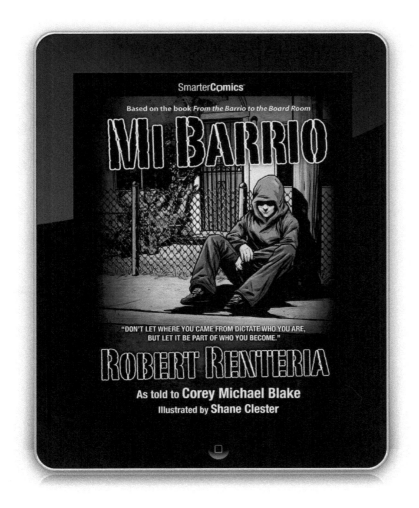

SmarterComics
Based on the book From the Barrio to the Board Room
MI BARRIO
"DON'T LET WHERE YOU CAME FROM DICTATE WHO YOU ARE, BUT LET IT BE PART OF WHO YOU BECOME."
ROBERT RENTERIA
As told to Corey Michael Blake
Illustrated by Shane Clester

CPSIA information can be obtained
at www.ICGtesting.com
Printed in the USA
JSHW062019280423
41032JS00001B/8

9 781610 660006